HOW TO GET STARTED IN VIDEO

HOW TO GET STARTED IN
VIDEO

DANIEL AND SUSAN COHEN

FRANKLIN WATTS
NEW YORK/LONDON/SYDNEY
TORONTO/1986

Photographs courtesy of: MTV (Music Television): pp. 10, 15; BET (Black Entertainment Television): p. 16; HBO (Home Box Office): pp. 27, 28; ESPN/Rick LaBranche: pp. 31, 37, 41; Emerson College: pp. 35, 80; CNN (Cable News Network): p. 38; Rich Tarbell: pp. 48, 58; Sony Corporation: p. 55; Johns Hopkins Children's Center (Baltimore, Maryland): p. 65; U.S. Department of Agriculture: p. 68; Syracuse University: pp. 75, 76, 79, 80, 83.

Library of Congress Cataloging in Publication Data

Cohen, Daniel.
How to get started in video.
Bibliography: p.
Includes index.
Summary: Discusses various career opportunities in television and video and how to prepare for and find a job in this field.
1. Television—Production and direction—Vocational guidance—Juvenile literature. 2. Video recordings—Production and direction—Vocational guidance—Juvenile literature. [1. Television—Production and direction—Vocational guidance. 2. Video recordings—Production and direction—Vocational guidance. 3. Vocational guidance] I. Cohen, Susan, 1938-   . II. Title
PN1992.75.C56   791.45′023   86-7751
ISBN 0-531-10250-5

Copyright © 1986 by Daniel and Susan Cohen
All rights reserved
Printed in the United States of America
6 5 4 3 2 1

CONTENTS

Chapter 1
The Look of the Future
9

Chapter 2
On the Cable
19

Chapter 3
In the Studio
34

Chapter 4
You Can Become
a TV Star
43

Chapter 5
Make Your Own Videos
53

Chapter 6
Video Everywhere
60

Chapter 7
Education in Video
71

Chapter 8
Where to Go from Here
86

Index
109

The authors would like to acknowledge
the cooperation of the following individuals
in helping us obtain information
and/or photographs for this book:

Lisa Wood, Emerson College; Joyce Tumbelston,
Marilyn Bentley, John Orentlicher, Syracuse University;
Mike Egan and Gary Susman,
Orange County, New York, Cablevision;
Steve Moore, UCLA;
Jane Weatheree, Turner Broadcasting;
Sherry Marsh, A&M Records;
Tamara Wells; Michael Collins; Jerry Kramer;
Dale Levitz, Johns Hopkins Medical School;
John McClung, U.S. Department of Agriculture;
Lt. Col. Fred Lynch, U.S. Air Force;
Maurice Higgins, Monroe Woodbury High School
AV Club, Orange County, New York.

CHAPTER ONE

THE LOOK OF THE FUTURE

You grab your remote, click on your TV, and keep switching channels till you hit MTV, Music Television. Then you stop. You're looking at one of MTV's VJs, (video jockeys), smiling out at you from the screen, relaxed, casual, friendly. As you watch, waiting for the next rock video, you can't help but think that being an MTV VJ must be a super job, one of the most glamorous in television, right up there with CBS's Dan Rather or Jane Pauley of "The Today Show" or even a famous talk-show host like Johnny Carson.

And it is true that MTV, the twenty-four-hour-a-day, seven-day-a-week rock music cable channel, is one of the most exciting recent developments in television, with the VJ the on-camera personification of the channel. Young, appealing, the VJ looks like someone you might know. The MTV set looks like a modern living room—not too fancy, not too plain. Just as the VJs

MTV VJs (front, left to right) Martha Quinn, Nina Blackwood; (rear, left to right) Alan Hunter, Mark Goodman, J. J. Jackson

themselves are attractive but not so attractive you feel you can't identify with them. They don't dazzle you. That's left to the rock stars.

Beyond the VJs and the performers in the music videos are a lot of people you don't see and never will. There are producers, directors, choreographers, writers, technicians who work with lighting and sound, people who do makeup, hairdressers, and camera operators. Beyond them are executives, secretaries, public relations personnel, accountants, and so forth. Go further yet and there are a variety of jobs at advertising agencies that produce the commercials you see between the music videos, sometimes as eye-catching as the videos themselves.

Yet before 1981 there was no MTV, and that really wasn't so very long ago. So video jockey is a new job category. But there is always something new and promising about television. That's why it's the field of the present and the future. Thanks to the expansion of cable TV and a host of other technological advances, video has grown in ways you may never have dreamed of. It's a good field in which to plan a career.

Video is used by corporations, at conventions and industrial shows. Department stores use video; so do hotels, even racetracks. Music videos are shown in video clubs. Stockbrokers use video. Video is used in schools, in museums, in hospitals, and by creative artists. Remember, too, it isn't so much where video is today as where it will be five or ten years from now. The video camera is as much a part of many teenagers' lives these days as a computer.

As noted California film and video director Michael Collins says, "I was eighteen when I got my first still camera. My son is only ten years old and he's already proficient with a video camera."

It's the technology that has expanded the field and has changed the way all of us see things. Probably nobody understands the video revolution better than you because you're young. You've grown up with it. You've helped make it happen. You've seen to it that along with technological changes have come changes in style. According to Collins, "Thanks to MTV, television is more visual than ever before."

Your generation responds to moods and impressions in a new way. On MTV the screen explodes with flashing images, quick bursts of information, what people in the ad agencies describe as a "nonlinear approach," abandoning transitions and connections. You are what CBS producer Tom Yellin calls "video fluent." Older people, who did not grow up with this style, are sometimes puzzled and resentful. But this pulsating, glittering style, with its bold graphics, has spread beyond MTV, influencing fashion, hairstyles, commercials, films—in short, what we see and how we look. Would rock films like *Flashdance* and *Purple Rain* have been such huge successes if music videos hadn't pointed the way? And what about the rat-a-tat rapid pacing of a lot of other kinds of movies targeted at a teen audience? Many of the standard network shows have been deeply influenced by the MTV style.

When it comes to audio, MTV has also had its effect. Before MTV, the recording industry was in a slump. But as people started watching videos on MTV they went out and bought records. That's just what the recording industry hoped they would do. Originally music videos were called "promos" and bands used them solely to promote records. But they have done more than sell records; they've evolved into their own art form, eclipsing records in importance.

Without music videos, without television itself, the world would never have been brought together as it was on July 13, 1985. On that date Live Aid proved that with satellites, television is the most sweeping yet immediate method of communication ever developed. A sixteen-hour rock telecast, carried in part by broadcast networks and in full by MTV, featured segments of rock concerts staged in London and Philadelphia. It's estimated that over a billion people around the world watched, and tens of millions of dollars were raised to feed the starving people in Africa. That event, dubbed "the Woodstock of the eighties"—a reference to the rock concert that seemed to embody the mood of the sixties—was an extraordinary technological achievement, bringing nations together. Who knows what other global events will be organized through television in the future?

But back to basics, and the basic observation is that there would have been no MTV without cable, and all that followed would never have happened. The reason is simple. Over-the-air, or broadcast, TV can only accommodate a dozen channels or less. If you're "on the cable" you can get twenty, thirty, or a hundred channels. Some other new technologies can also vastly increase the number of available channels, but more of that later. A broadcast network must have as wide an appeal as possible. But when you have to please everybody, that may mean bland fare. A cable channel, which is only one of many, can have a much narrower appeal and still succeed.

As a cable channel MTV could afford to be different. It was for a limited age group, officially twelve to thirty-five, and you certainly fit in there somewhere. MTV abandoned the standard program format. Whether you watched MTV at breakfast time, noon, or in the middle of the night you saw the same fare—rock videos.

Yet from this seemingly formless format MTV developed some extremely original and innovative programming ideas, such as encouraging viewers to link up with stereo. A few television stations, particularly public television, had tried the stereo linkup, but before MTV, sound was TV's second-class citizen. Now stereo TVs are hot items.

Through a heavy advertising campaign involving T-shirts, a cleverly designed logo, and a real sense of what teenagers wanted, MTV was turned into a successful pioneer channel, a phenomenon in the television business.

MTV urged viewers to phone in, cast votes for their favorite rock videos, express their opinions, stay in touch, really feel that the channel was their own. No broadcast network could create this kind of intimate time, this viewer loyalty.

A video awards show was created, along with specials, concerts, interviews with rock stars, documentaries, and tons of music news. MTV announces the dates of rock concerts and tells you where and when tickets go on sale, sponsors concerts, shows taped live concerts, offers weekend specials, provides you with a behind-the-scenes look at how videos are made, and even shows classic cult films and music-oriented films like *Rock Rock Rock.*

There are "Friday Night Video Fights," where rock videos compete for viewer votes and you choose the winner. "Basement Tapes" gives unknown singers and bands a chance to reach a wide audience. New performers send in tapes. A panel of experts picks a group of the best, and the MTV audience picks a winner, who receives a recording contract, several thousand dollars' worth of equipment, and an opportunity to make another music video. There are incredible and really original contests. Viewers have won everything from a pink house to a weekend with Van Halen.

Even people who don't like MTV acknowledge that its enormous success has changed television forever.

All of this is light-years away from MTV's humble beginnings on August 1, 1981. The crowd of people

MTV MUSIC TELEVISION™

Video Soul on Black Entertainment Television

who filed into a Fort Lee, New Jersey, restaurant that night worked for the Warner/Amex Satellite Entertainment Company, parent company of MTV. Though they cheered loudly when MTV appeared on the half-dozen television sets in the restaurant, nobody knew for sure whether they were witnessing the birth of a great new channel or another dud. After all, there had been other cable channels, and many of them had flopped. The reason the crowd was in New Jersey was because you couldn't get MTV in New York City where the Warner/Amex employees worked. Only four million homes, a tiny number for a television audience, could get MTV at all at the start. Today MTV reaches over twenty-seven million cable subscribers, and the number is growing. MTV was an idea whose time had come, and as the Buggles's "Video Killed the Radio Star" (the first music video ever shown on the channel) lit up the screen, television history was made.

Rapidly rock videos reached other cable channels like the USA network which boasts "Radio 1990" and "Night Flight." MTV spawned another music video network, VH-1, which is aimed at older audiences. Country music videos have begun appearing on those channels that specialize in country music. Even the broadcast networks got into the act with regular music video programs. Local channels have their own video shows, sometimes featuring local bands. All of this, of course, has opened a vast new area for careers. But only the boldest would have predicted this sort of explosive development back in 1981, and that wasn't so long ago.

What else is on the video horizon? What does it mean to you and your future career? The changes have come so quickly that it's hard to predict accurately. One thing is for sure, there will be more jobs. There are only a few VJs today, maybe there will be many more VJs on local channels tomorrow. There are certainly going to be thousands of other jobs.

MTV and the big networks have all the glamour, but don't scorn the small, the local, and the less glamorous side of video. No matter what your goals, you have to start somewhere, you have to learn your trade, and you have to develop a taste for hard work. Tamara Wells, who has produced music videos featuring stars like John Waite, Iron Maiden, and Eric Clapton, says, "Production and creative jobs aren't all glamour. They're hard work. You must work hard once you're a success just to survive."

Whether you want to struggle your way to the top or seek a lifetime job with less pressure, you must begin at the beginning, and that means getting good all-around training and experience. So before you reach for the stars, be practical and look at the kind of job you can reach for and get when you start out.

CHAPTER TWO
ON THE CABLE

The studios for Orange County Cablevision's local cable channel are located in a squat brick building atop a hill outside of the small city of Middletown, New York. In appearance the building is utterly unlike the gleaming steel-and-glass mid-Manhattan towers that are the headquarters for the major networks.

Orange County Cablevision has a single production facility with a handful of employees. The company's main business is supplying its area's subscribers with coaxial cable so that they not only get better reception of the broadcast networks but can also receive cable networks such as HBO, Showtime, MTV, and ESPN. Cablevision also operates its own local channel, Cable 6. Programming on Cable 6 is limited. The only regular locally produced feature is a half-hour news show that runs five days a week. There are also sports shows, broadcasts of local high school football and basketball games, and occasional specials. In addition there are a variety of syndicated shows which are purchased rather than produced locally. Currently one of the most popular is the syndicated "International Championship Wrestling." The Cable 6 staff also makes commercials for local advertisers. These ads are shown not only on the local channel but are inserted in specially allotted spots in MTV, ESPN, and other commercial cable networks in the company's area.

It's a small operation and a far cry from the multimillion-dollar glamour associated with CBS, NBC, and ABC.

And that's just the way Cable 6's producer-director, Calvin DeMond, whose first job had been with one of the major networks, likes it.

"What's a producer-director?" we asked him.

"That means jack-of-all-trades," he replied, smiling.

On the day we visited with DeMond, he was screening a commercial that he had made to advertise the Orange County Fair.

"I *really* made that commercial," he said with pride. "I wrote the script, I shot it, I edited it, I even did the voice-over. The commercial sometimes runs on the big New York City channels, and when I see it I always get the biggest kick, because it's all mine.

"When I worked for the network I was making good money, but I felt that I was being confined in a narrow technical area. I was a good technician, but I didn't get a chance to do anything else. I couldn't learn anything new. Here I learn all the time. You have to improvise. A small station like this is a good place to start."

And there are hundreds of small operations like Cable 6 throughout the country.

We asked DeMond how he thought a young person interested in getting into television or video might get started.

"The first thing to do is see if you can visit your local TV station. You don't have to understand what's going on. Just see if you like the atmosphere—the feel of the place. See if it seems like the sort of place where you would like to work. If it feels right, that's a good first step.

"Then go to the library and read up on television. You don't have to read the technical stuff. You can find out about the history. Read about Edward R. Murrow and David Sarnoff and Ernie Kovacs. Find out the differences between cable and over-the-air TV. It's interesting and it will give you something to talk about with TV people.

"Volunteer. A small station like this often needs help. Even if it's just sweeping the floor and getting coffee for the news department, volunteering puts you in the building. You meet the people, and you can learn a lot by just watching. You'll also know more about whether it's the sort of work you want to do.

"If you have a public television station in your area, call them. Public TV is strapped for funds and always needs free help. You might start by answering phones during a fund drive. As I said, it doesn't make any difference what you do at first—the important thing is that it puts you where television is being made. You get a chance to meet the people who are making it."

As a teenager, DeMond was fascinated by television. But he didn't have his own video camera. "I didn't even own a still camera." His introduction to television came through a high school class. It wasn't a particularly advanced or well-equipped class, but an enthusiastic teacher kept his interest alive and growing. By the time he got to college, he found that he had picked up so much in high school that many of his courses were a breeze. "I definitely recommend college to anyone thinking of going into television," he says.

Another thing he recommends is interning—working for free at a TV station while in college. An intern is more likely to get hands-on experience than a volunteer. Sometimes colleges or even high schools can arrange internships; other times it's up to the student to find one. But DeMond stresses that they are important. Not only do you learn a lot, but people who do the hiring often get a chance to see what you can do. DeMond himself was hired by ABC after interning there.

He admits that he was lucky to be in the right place at the right time, that the networks are hard to crack except at the lowest level jobs. He believes it's harder to start at a network now than it was when he got his first job. "It's really best to start at a small station where you can learn the whole business."

Down the hall from DeMond's office is Cable 6's modest newsroom where news director Tracy Baxter was doing some paperwork. Baxter is not only the news director, he is one-half of the entire news department. The other half is young Marianne Worley, who was editing the tape of a story that she had covered earlier in the day.

Though Cable 6 has only one half-hour newscast five days a week, preparing that thirty minutes is a full-time job for Baxter and Worley.

"We cover only local news," says Baxter. "The networks and the New York City stations cover the international, national, and even statewide news. Our job is to get what they don't.

"We generate the vast majority of stories on our own. We get press releases or phone calls from people who tell us about events that they think are newsworthy. We cover as many of them as we can."

He pointed to a police scanner radio perched atop a file cabinet. "We listen to that all day. If something important comes up we get there. We also check with police agencies regularly, and with the various local governments."

Baxter, who came over to television from local radio news, knows the area well. As DeMond had done, Baxter emphasized that at a small station you get involved in all phases of the work. "You cover the stories, write your own copy, edit the tape, and appear on camera during the broadcast." Unlike larger stations where there are correspondents in the field and an anchor at a desk in the studio, Baxter and Worley do both.

When covering stories they are usually accompanied by a camera operator, but on occasion Baxter has lugged the equipment all by himself, and interviewed subjects while running the camera. It's a job that seems to require at least one extra set of hands.

Interns supplied by journalism departments of nearby colleges or willing volunteers are welcomed by the small, often overburdened news staff. "They help supplement us on news shoots; they learn to run the cameras; they even do some interviewing after a while. It's a good way to start. A couple of our regular cameramen started as interns or volunteers."

But he stressed that, generally, for television news work a degree in broadcast journalism was essential. "While at school you should work with the college station or a local TV station for experience," he said.

Worley was a recent graduate of the Newhouse School of Public Communications at Syracuse University. She also believes that being part of a small operation allows you, indeed forces you, to become involved in all phases of television news.

Producers, directors, the people who read the news, and those who run the cameras—those are the obvious jobs at a cable television station. But there are lots of others, from secretaries and bookkeepers to advertising sales people. So long as you work in the studio there is always a chance of moving around and moving up.

An entirely different aspect of the cable system and the jobs it may provide was given by Orange County Cablevision's systems manager, Mike Egan. Egan doesn't work out of Cable 6's studio, but out of the system's main office in Liberty, New York.

Egan is not primarily concerned with developing programming, but rather with receiving the signals from cable and broadcast networks, and having them delivered via cable to the homes of individual subscribers. Selling the service to subscribers is the moneymaking end of the cable business.

There is a technical staff; from the engineers who oversee the sophisticated equipment that receives the signals often bounced off the satellites (the place where the signals are received and processed is called the headend); to the cable installers who actually run the cable into the subscribers' homes, hook it up to their TV sets, and make sure that it stays hooked up properly.

Installer is the entry-level job. You don't need a college degree. A special course, even a correspondence course, can provide the necessary training, says Egan.

Installers, however, need some special talents. They can't be afraid of heights, because they have to spend a lot of time climbing poles to string wire. And since they have to go into people's homes to hook up (or occasionally disconnect) the equipment, they have to be good at public relations as well. People take their televisions very personally, so if they've been having problems with the cable, some customers are likely to be somewhat irritable and need careful and courteous handling.

Starting as an installer an individual can, with experience and additional training, move up the technical ladder in a cable company. There are line technicians, service technicians, and, back at the repair facility, there are bench technicians who fix broken or malfunctioning equipment. Engineers working at the headend generally need college training in engineering. In many smaller systems a two-year associate's degree in an appropriate technical area is sufficient.

There are a variety of technical jobs involved in the actual construction of a cable system, but these, Egan points out, are really a separate kind of career.

In the central office there are marketing and advertising jobs. Marketing in a cable system has become increasingly specialized and sophisticated, and a job of marketing director often requires an advanced degree in broadcasting administration, or business marketing. The marketing staff sells the cable company's service to the community. They also try to keep up with which channels their subscribers want, and which they don't want.

As with any other office the central office of a cable company has secretaries, bookkeepers, customer service representatives, and so on.

Usually the central office and the programming side of cable are quite separate. A line technician does not have the same sort of skills as a camera operator or editor, though both are technical jobs. But one area where the two sides of cable overlap is advertising.

Advertising is a fairly new aspect of cable television. Local advertisers often want to see their own ads on some of the major cable networks such as ESPN or MTV as well as on whatever local programs the cable system offers. The advertising staff must not only sell the ads, but also work with the production side of the business to develop the ad.

Orange County Cablevision is only one representative, and a small one, of the cable TV industry which has sometimes been called the fastest-growing entertainment industry in America. Yet, with features like the Cable News Network, the Weather Channel, and a flock of local news shows, cable is a lot broader than entertainment alone. It's a big industry and a growing one. It's also a confusing one. Newton Minow, a longtime influential figure in television, once quipped that only three people understood cable TV; "One is dead, one is insane, and I refuse to talk about it." It's not quite that bad.

Many people regard cable TV as a new technology. Actually it's been around since 1948. It was called CATV then—Community Antenna Television. Cable began as a service for areas where the reception of broadcast TV was poor. The cable operator picked up the signals with a large antenna and delivered them to the houses of the subscribers via a cable, like a telephone line. For the advantage of getting a good picture, or sometimes any TV picture at all, the subscriber paid a modest fee. Many of the cable systems were very small, operated by a local TV repair service or store that sold TVs. They came to be called "mom-and-pop cable systems."

That's pretty much the way cable remained until the early 1970s when Home Box Office (HBO) was formed with the idea of sending uncut and uninterrupted movies into the homes of subscribers. For this service they were charged an additional fee.

The real explosion in cable TV came in the mid-seventies when the potential of communications satellites was realized. A signal could be sent up to a satellite and be retransmitted down to special antennas at individual cable companies all over the country. The companies then sent the signals into the homes of subscribers via cable. This development made cable networks not only possible but potentially profitable. The great advantage to cable is that while over-the-air TV can handle a mere dozen channels, cable is capable of handling over a hundred.

*The HBO satellite communications center
at Hauppauge, Long Island, New York*

The master control room at the HBO satellite communications center

Soon a variety of cable networks had sprung up. Some, like HBO, relied primarily on movies. Others offered specialized content, like all-news or all-sports programs. On broadcast TV there would have been no room for a twenty-four-hour-a-day music video network. But with a huge number of available channels, such a network could be set up, and many have been. In extremes of program content, cable networks range from the Christian Broadcasting Network to the Playboy Channel.

Once the cable-satellite connection had been made, cable TV leaped from being a nickel-and-dime operation serving primarily rural areas to something that everybody wanted. Not only did cable give people better reception, it gave them a lot of things that they couldn't get on broadcast TV, and people were willing to pay for that.

Each community licenses its own cable system, and since a cable TV franchise can be extremely profitable, the competition for franchises can be fierce. Each community also sets its own regulations, and each cable system supplies different services to its subscribers. Some cable operators are small and independent, but increasingly huge multiple-system operators, owned by such corporate giants as General Electric and Warner/Amex, have dominated, particularly in the large urban markets.

Still, cable TV across the United States is a crazy quilt, and an ever-changing one, of companies, services, and regulations.

There are a lot more jobs with local cable systems than with the big cable networks which originate many of the programs. This is particularly true for newcomers. The Cable News Network hires only experienced correspondents, and it is doubtful if a newcomer could get much on-the-job engineering training at the sophisticated HBO transmission center at Hauppauge, New York. Some cable networks rely primarily on movies or even reruns of old network TV shows, and do little if any original programming. Still there is no doubt that the cable networks have opened up a huge area of new careers.

While cable TV has grown explosively over the last few years, and its possibilities seem almost unlimited, there are some clouds on the horizon, so a few words of caution are necessary.

To hear some cable TV enthusiasts talk you would think that pretty soon every television set in America will be receiving a hundred channels via cable. But in fact, cable operators have discovered that even when given a choice of a couple dozen channels, there are some that are never, or almost never, watched. Quite a number of cable networks have failed because they couldn't attract a large enough audience to become profitable. Others are in serious financial trouble. Some cable operators have cut back on plans to offer additional channels because not enough people seem to want them.

Some cable operators believe that there is only a temporary pause in the expansion of cable channels, and maybe they're right. But there has been a pause nonetheless.

What once seemed to be one of the brightest promises of cable—interactive, or two-way, television—has also been disappointing. With two-way television the subscriber could order a particular movie, register an opinion in a poll, or buy something that was being shown on TV, just by pressing buttons on a keypad. The technology for interactive television exists. The possibilities seemed endless. Yet when the system was tested in the mid-1980s, it flopped, and the company that conducted the test lost a lot of money. Subscribers

ESPN's master control room

liked the system, but they didn't like it well enough to pay a substantial extra fee to use it. The test failure scared away a lot of other companies that were thinking of going into interactive TV. Once again, the pause may be only temporary. If interactive TV ever does catch on, the impact it will have on the cable industry will be monumental.

The number of homes within the reach of some sort of cable system is still expanding. Soon over 80 percent of American homes will potentially be "on the cable." More and more subscribers are signing up. Maybe they don't want a hundred channels, or two-way television, but they still do want a lot of what cable offers. Another way to pick up a large number of channels is with a dish antenna. If a person owns one he can pick up what cable has to offer directly from the satellite, without getting a cable hookup, and without paying the cable company fee. There are some legal qualifications, and satellite antennas are expensive, though the price has been dropping fast. For a while the satellite antennas were common only in areas so sparsely populated that it wasn't economically feasible to lay cable. But since the price of the antennas has been coming down, the antennas have been sprouting in areas serviced by cable companies—and the companies, while not panicked, are concerned, and are developing technology to meet this challenge. Major cable networks are now "scrambling" their signals so that they cannot be used by the ordinary satellite antenna owner.

Another system called DSB—Direct Satellite Broadcast—is currently being tested. With DSB all that is needed is a relatively small dish antenna, one that can sit on a windowsill rather than dominate the entire front yard. Right now the experimental DSB systems can receive only a handful of channels, but systems with larger capacity are on the drawing boards.

Cable TV, like all high-tech areas, is changing constantly, often in ways that are quite unexpected. If you're thinking about a career in cable in a few years, try to keep up with the changes. The more you know about what's happening in the industry the better prepared you'll be to take advantage of it.

CHAPTER THREE

IN THE STUDIO

While there are a huge number of jobs in a wide variety of areas related to video, when most people think of working in television they think about working in a television studio. In this chapter we're going to take a look at some of the studio jobs. It doesn't make any difference whether you are working in a cable studio or a broadcast studio, the jobs are the same. The difference is not in how the programs are produced, but how they are transmitted.

The most obvious jobs are those that are in front of the cameras. We've already discussed VJs as a new job category, and news reporters as being one of the more promising areas. Another familiar figure in TV stations large and small is the sportscaster or sports reporter.

The sports reporter is obviously a reporter who specializes in sports. This is a more difficult area to

TV studio at Emerson College

break into than news because there are fewer positions available—a channel may have four news reporters and only one sportscaster. Besides, lots of people want the job. The big-name network sportscasters are often retired athletes, which further cuts down the number of positions available. Still, a person who is knowledgeable in all areas of sports and looks and sounds good has a chance to break in on the local level. Even small cable channels often have regular sportscasters.

Local news shows often have a weather forecaster. Occasionally such an individual needs training in meteorology, but on most smaller channels it's strictly a matter of personality. In addition there are the people who host local interview shows and local game shows. Once again, on-screen personality is the key here, and these are rarely entry-level jobs. A good voice may land a person a job as an announcer.

Performers on television face the same challenges and difficulties as performers in films and on the stage; there are too many people competing for a relatively small number of jobs. Local stations rarely produce their own dramatic series, but trained performers sometimes serve as hosts or emcees on local shows. Most drama schools offer some special training for acting in television.

If you happen to live in an area where TV shows or commercials are often shot, it might be possible to pick up a bit part, even as a face in a crowd. Show business trade papers like *Variety* sometimes list casting calls for extras. This can be fun, and you can make some money at it, but being part of a crowd scene is rarely the road to stardom. However, we do know one seventy-year-old woman who started out picking up bit parts in commercials because she was retired and had nothing to do, and wound up being a nationwide celebrity. So lightning does strike sometimes, but you can't count on it.

ESPN's audio booth and production control room

Main studio for CNN, Cable News Network

A lot of people in television, particularly those who work behind the cameras, start as production assistants. It's often a poorly paid first job, and in some small operations the production assistants may be volunteers. It's the job of the production assistant to take care of all those details that other, more experienced members of the crew don't have time for, or simply don't want to bother with; which can be anything from holding cue cards to moving lights.

You can't shoot a television show without cameras, and so camera operators are always necessary. Even small stations usually have at least two for every show, and camera operators are needed for on-location shoots as well. Many camera operators begin as production assistants, but it's also very helpful to have some previous training with the equipment. Sheer physical strength may be a qualification as well, particularly for on-location shoots when the operator has to carry his or her own equipment.

A next step up the ladder can be floor manager. It's the floor manager's job to actually direct the traffic on the studio floor or at a remote location, during rehearsals and actual production. The floor manager has to make sure that everything—equipment, props, and performers—are all where they're supposed to be. If you look at a TV studio during production, the floor manager is generally the person with the headphones, frantically signaling to others on the set.

The voice the floor manager hears through the headphones is that of the director. The director is usually involved in a show from the planning stage, collaborating with producers and writers. During rehearsals and production the director oversees all production and engineering personnel from the control room, and communicates with the studio via headphones. He or she selects the camera shots and movements that will eventually be seen by the audience. If a show is to be taped, it's the director who oversees the editing. Directing is one of the most demanding and highly skilled jobs in television. Most directors get their positions by moving up through the ranks.

Depending on the size of the studio there can be many other people at work—assistant directors, unit managers, lighting directors, and so on. The full range of jobs is available only in the large studios. (Read all the credits that run at the end of a major television production. That will give you some idea of the large number of people involved.) In the small studios like those of Cable 6, people double and triple up on jobs.

A host of other technical people are needed to successfully operate even a moderate-size station. There is, for example, the audio/video engineer who is responsible for operating the electronic audio and video equipment in the control room. Another type of technician, the videotape engineer, has the job of setting up and operating all types of videotape machines, and for recording, playback, and editing. He or she is also in charge of the evaluation of videotapes, the duplication of taped material, and the assembling of videotapes for production and broadcast. Videotape engineers record programs being produced in the studios at their stations or those from outside sources. They also assemble and edit commercials, promotional spots, and station breaks. In short, if it has to do with videotape, and practically everything in modern television does, the videotape engineer may have a hand in it.

There are a lot of nontechnical jobs that you might not think of at first. Take writers, for example. A TV writer needs special visually oriented skills. There are graphic artists; someone has to design the title cards, the charts, the graphs, and all the other visual aids seen on TV. Graphic artists may also work preparing promotional material for the channel. There are other kinds of

ESPN's master control room

artists—makeup artists, hair stylists, and scene and costume designers.

If you've watched the credits on a film you may have noticed that down near the end there may be a credit for somebody as "grip." Perhaps you've wondered what a "grip" is. It's the person who moves the scenery and equipment from one place to another, and generally does everything that he or she can to make sure that things are where they are supposed to be. In theater, the person who does this sort of work is called a stagehand. In a TV studio either term can be used. Being a grip doesn't take any particular training, but many people regard a job like this as a good place to start. In small operations the work of the grip or stagehand, like the work of the production assistant, is often done by part-timers or volunteers.

This gives you some idea of the types of jobs that are available in the most obvious part of the television industry, the studio. There are, of course, many types of jobs beyond the studio, and a lot of jobs in video that are not directly connected with what we normally think of as the TV industry.

If you've ever watched a TV production being shot, particularly by one of the larger companies, the overwhelming impression one gets is that it takes an enormous number of people to make the operation work. Someday one of those people may be you.

CHAPTER FOUR

YOU CAN BECOME A TV STAR

You can star in your own TV show. Or you can produce and direct your own show and get it on television. You can do it now, and for free—or nearly so—if you're lucky. By being lucky we mean that you have to live near a cable system that has a local access channel.

Remember we said that cable franchises operate under a patchwork of different rules, regulations, and services. Each system has to negotiate a contract with the local government. Since the contracts are highly competitive, cable companies often try to prove that they will be good citizens by offering the community various services—one of them might be a public-access channel.

A public-access channel is different from a local cable channel like Cable 6 which we described in an earlier chapter. Cable 6 and others like it are local *origination* channels. Such channels may show local news, or even locally produced shows. But the management of the channel has complete control over what goes on. Cable companies may also lease a channel, or a specified time portion, for the purpose of airing programs with a commercial theme, or programs with a sponsor. The buyer then takes responsibility for the content of whatever is shown on the leased channel or time. Those tiresomely long shows that tell you how to become a millionaire selling real estate or vitamin supplements are examples of this sort of leasing.

The public-access channel is quite different. Practically anyone who has anything to say or show can walk into an access channel station and get on TV. And it can all be free or available at a very low cost—the studio time, the use of the equipment, the services of trained personnel, as well as the on-the-air time. Moreover, in some areas the cable company will actually train people in how to use the equipment and produce shows—again it's all free, or available for a nominal fee.

In their purest form public-access channels are democracy in action. And that's what they're supposed to be. It's mass media that can become everybody's media. There may be as many as fifteen hundred access channels in the nation. They are more likely to be found in newer and larger transmitting systems with a large number of channels available, than in older systems with limited capacity.

Now it's not all that rosy. Cable systems operators may be 100 percent for democracy, personally. But the systems are supposed to be profit making. They offer free access and training only in order to gain the goodwill of the local authorities who make the decisions about franchising. Access doesn't make the cable company any money; indeed they lose money on the deal. An access channel may make a few people in a community more willing to subscribe to a cable service, but this is by no means certain. And access channels can be troublesome as well. We'll explain how in a moment. So a lot of cable systems are not very eager to let the public know what's available to them even when they do have an access channel.

Public access TV may be one of the most underutilized natural resources in the nation. It will remain underutilized unless and until the public wakes up to its potential and gets involved.

If you don't know whether or not there is a public-access channel in your area, call the headquarters of your local cable company and find out. If you have a video class in school the instructor might know. High schools and colleges often have close contact with access channels. In some areas the schools actually control the access channel.

We mentioned that public-access television sometimes can be troublesome and controversial. If anybody can get on access television and say and do anything, then you are likely to get some pretty strange programs. And that's just exactly what happened. The first cable franchise to offer public access was Manhattan Cable TV. Its charter franchise is probably the most liberal in the nation. According to Manhattan Cable, "To assure maximum opportunity for freedom of expression by members of the public, programming on the public channels shall be free from any control by the Company as to program content. . . ." The hope was for free and open discussion; the result was shows like "Midnight Blue" and "The Ugly George Hour of Truth, Sex and Violence," which was just exactly what it sounds like. These became famous, indeed notorious, throughout the nation. They contained material that would be banned from the Playboy Channel. The controversy gave a lot of people the impression that public-access television was mainly pornography. That impression is quite false. Most public-access channels do have controls imposed on them either by the cable company or by the city or county government that franchised the company. What can and can't go on the air varies a great deal. Most cable systems demand that programs conform to "community standards"—this is very general, but it means the shows shouldn't make a lot of people angry or upset. Obscene material is not acceptable in most systems, and it is doubtful if a person like Ugly George could get on even Manhattan Cable TV anymore. In some places restrictions on public access are very great indeed.

A lot of public-access TV is amateurish and just plain boring. Access channels have been used to broadcast city council meetings, interviews with the sewer commissioner, or talks by somebody who has an idea that no one else understands or wants to hear about. You can't get more boring than that. But it has occasionally produced programs that are fresh, innovative, and a lot better than much of the fare on commercial television. Most of all, an access cable channel is a great way to start getting some TV experience. So if there's one close by, take advantage of your good fortune.

How can public-access TV be useful to you? First, there's the workshop or training session. These are usually run by the cable company or whatever community group controls the access channel, and they're usually free. If they do cost something it's minimal, and that's a price you can't beat. While the quality of training varies, and you won't be able to step into a network job after a few training sessions, the novice is sure to learn something and get a chance to handle the equipment.

Then there is volunteer work. As we've noted, public-access TV is very much the unwanted stepchild of cable television. The cable companies put up with it, but they don't really want to spend money on it. So the studios are likely to be severely understaffed and any responsible help will be welcomed. With a little luck at all you may soon find yourself running a camera, handling the sound, directing interview shows, and getting into almost all phases of production. You will be able to get more responsibility more quickly because your services will be needed.

You won't get paid a penny, but the experience can be invaluable, and the work can be great fun because the *esprit de corps* in many access channels is tremendous. Sometimes working at an access channel can lead directly to a job because there are some cable systems operators who use the access channel as a recruiting pool. The managers can see people at work. The volunteer is also in a better position to hear about jobs that might be available in his or her local cable system or others.

But let's say that you don't just want to work in the studio, but that you want to produce your own show— or perhaps star in it. You can do that, too, but it takes a willingness to work hard and again you need luck.

You have to start by getting in touch with the coordinator of your local access channel, or anyone else at the studio who can tell you about it. Find out what the requirements are for getting a show on the channel. Some channels are hardly used, and management is looking for something—almost anything—to fill the time. Others are very popular, and there's a waiting list of shows. The management of such channels can afford to be pretty choosy. And there are those who are just going through the motions of offering an access channel, and don't want to bother with you at all.

Find out what the facilities are. Can you do a live show in the studio? Can you tape one? Be sure to ask about cost. We said that most public-access TV is free, but some stations will charge a nominal fee for use of the studio, for tape, or for airtime. There is no nationwide standard, and cable companies are constantly revising their policies. So be sure that you know what

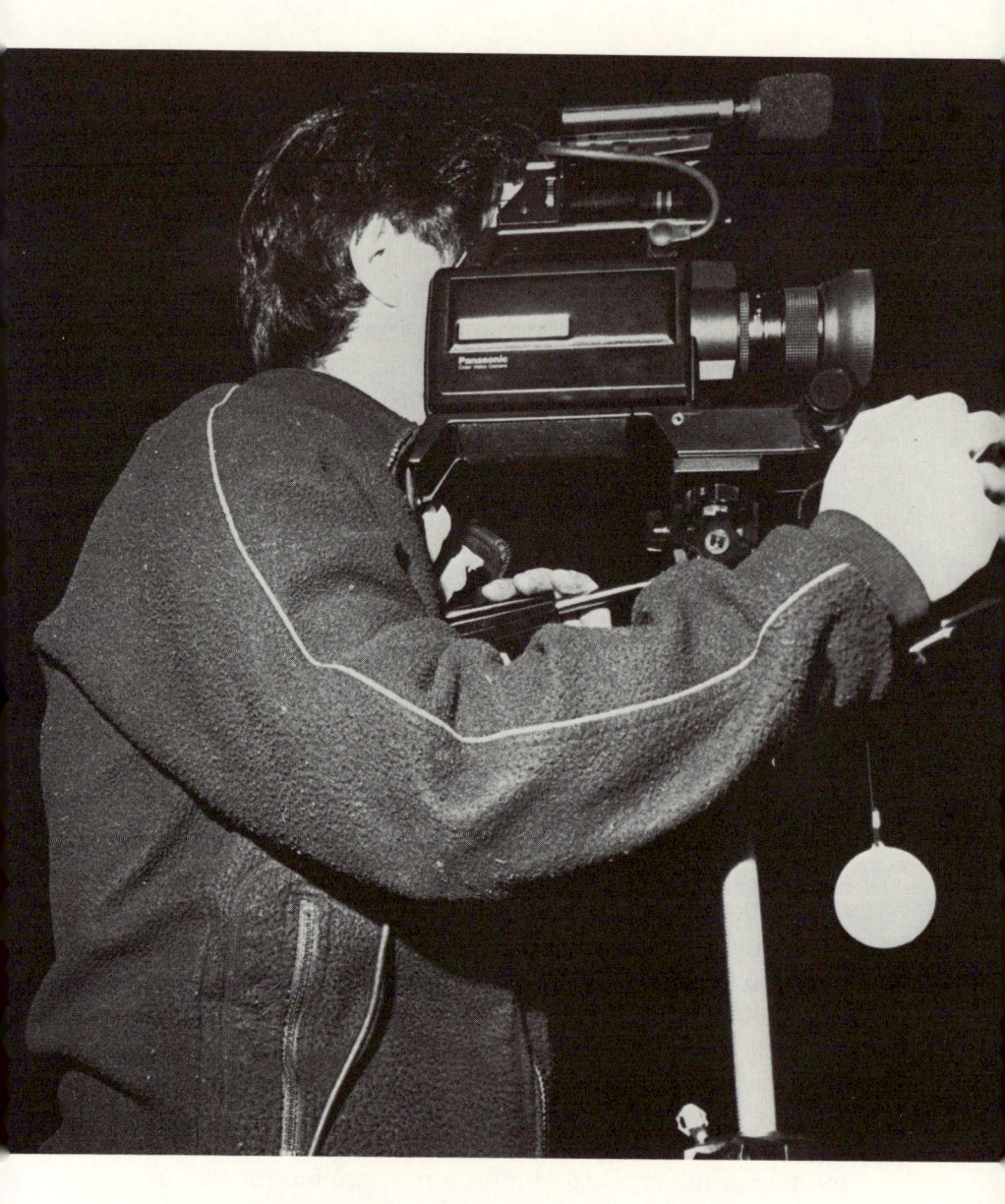

Working at a cable access channel will give the volunteer an opportunity to become familiar with video equipment.

you are getting into. Access in major areas like New York or Los Angeles is going to cost more than access in a small town.

Ellen Stern Harris, who is vice-president of the Public Access Producers Association, says, "Access channels on cable systems can be the twentieth-century equivalent of open space and parks. Access channels, as well as parks, provide the spaces people need to explore, to exchange ideas with people they've never met before, to share their experiences and talents—to let one another know what's happening in the neighborhood and the region. People have got to know that they have an 'in' to community television. It can work for anybody who wants to give it a try."

So you want to put your own show on television. That's fine. But first you better have a solid idea of what sort of a show it's going to be, and you had better be able to explain it clearly to the access coordinator or whoever is in charge of what gets shown. Just wanting to be on TV isn't enough.

In any area your show will have a better chance of getting on the air if it has a news or community service element to it. Let's say that in your town there is a community project to raise funds to restore the old downtown railroad station which has fallen into disrepair. You could interview the people who are sponsoring the project—they would probably be glad to talk to you. You could show old photographs of the station as it was and drawings of how it is hoped that it will be. You might also insert a videotape of the station as it is now, pointing out the features that will be repaired and restored. You might also include live or taped interviews with old-timers who remember the station in the days of its glory.

We grant that such a project would not make the most exciting television in the world. But it would be a complex and ambitious undertaking for a newcomer, so you could learn a lot. It's also the sort of project that would look good when mentioned on any college entrance form or application for financial aid. A videotape of such a show could be submitted as an example of your work.

Besides, if people knew that the show was going to be on they might watch. Local cable shows do get an audience, and there is a great deal of satisfaction when someone comes up to you on the street and says, "Hey, I saw you on TV."

An entertainment program is another possibility. Some access shows have featured local bands or even comedy sketches written and performed by local talent. It's a little harder to get this sort of show on the air. Entertainment does not have an obvious public service or educational value. Then you must convince the access coordinator that the show really will be entertaining, not just a bunch of kids mugging and goofing around. Public-access television is often amateurish, but it tries not to be *that* amateurish.

If you're dreaming that your access show will suddenly become a big hit and result in a big contract from one of the commercial channels, don't abandon the dream, but don't count on it, either. A couple of cable access "superstars" have struck it—if not big—at least pretty big, but instant success stories are rare indeed.

Karen Salkin, an eccentric but unemployed actress, did a show called "Karen's Restaurant Revue" (which had little to do with restaurants and a lot to do with Karen's funny, strange, high-speed monologues) on an access channel in Los Angeles. Just by chance Johnny Carson saw her show, liked her, and booked her for several guest slots on "The Tonight Show." It was a great break.

Arnie Rosenthal moved from the producer and host of an access cable game show to being a TV entrepreneur. Rosenthal managed to sell local advertising on his Manhattan-based access show "The Big Giveaway"—the giveaway wasn't that big—he started the show with a nest egg of seven hundred dollars. Many access channels will not allow the sale of advertising, but as with just about everything else about access cable, there are no universally applicable rules. Rosenthal's show was picked up by other cable systems. From the experience and contacts he gained while doing "The Big Giveaway," Rosenthal was able to buy shows produced in Europe and sell them as a package to various cable channels and networks and even some over-the-air channels. The Rosenthal package, called "The English Channel," was a major financial success.

But as we said, such tales of success are rare. Access cable is far more likely to be a stepping stone than a launching pad.

But what if you've got a local show that you really think deserves national attention? There are a couple of cable networks that are in need of programming, and occasionally—only occasionally—will take a show from an unknown. It's a long shot—like a totally unknown writer sending a story off to *The New Yorker*—but if you've got something that you think is really good, and it has good production values, you might want to gamble. Don't just send in a tape; write first, find out if the network is interested in what you have and what the requirements are. A warning: even if one of the cable networks does accept your show they won't pay you, and you may have to pay them. A listing of the largest cable networks will be found at the back of this book.

A less ambitious but more practical way of getting your work greater exposure is by establishing your own regional "network." Some locally produced shows would be of interest in neighboring areas as well. Local sports shows are what seem to do best. If you think you have such a show, find out what other local access or local origination channels are in the area. Someone at your cable channel might know, or the local library might have a directory like the *Cable Fact Book*. Call up some nearby systems and see if they're interested. If they have a local channel with airtime to fill they just might be. If it's a local origination channel rather than a local access channel, the operator might feel that some money could be made from selling advertising on your show. Don't expect that you're going to make any money at first, or ever. You're in it for the exposure.

If you can get several systems interested in the show, you can engage in the practice known as bicycling. Arrange to have the tape sent from one system to the next, rather than being returned to you first; it saves on the cost of making extra tapes and it saves on postage. Some cable systems have begun sharing or exchanging locally produced programs with nearby systems. This sort of cooperation can work to the advantage of everyone concerned.

But let's get back to basics before you are carried away by visions of your own cable TV network and, following in the footsteps of another cable magnate, challenging for the leadership of CBS. Remind yourself that money—let alone big money—is almost unknown in access television. At best it's an outlet for the free exchange of ideas and a showcase for new talent. Sometimes it's little more than Vanity Video.

Whatever it is, it's a great place to start. If the opportunity is there for you, you should take advantage of it.

CHAPTER FIVE

MAKE YOUR OWN VIDEOS

The VCR, video cassette recorder, has become a familiar and cherished item in American households. It was first introduced into the American market in 1975, but because of the prohibitive price it remained a luxury item until the early 1980s. Then prices began dropping fast, and the VCR became just about the hottest selling consumer item around. Not every American home has a VCR; the price, which hovers around three hundred dollars, is still too steep for many. But millions have been sold, and millions more are being sold every year. Soon few homes will be without one. The VCR has revolutionized television viewing in this country, and it's opened a whole new area for jobs—the sale and rental of video software, that is, tapes. Video stores have been popping up like mushrooms after a rain. It's a new and expanding branch of retailing.

But the VCR will bring about other changes, for if a VCR is in the home, can a video camera be far behind? While sales of video cameras still lag well behind sales of VCRs, they, too, are increasing, and the end certainly is not in sight.

The home video camera has largely replaced the home movie camera. It's simpler to operate. Tape is cheaper than film, and it's reusable. But most important of all, you don't have to wait to have the film developed. All you have to do is stick the tape in the VCR to see what you've got. If you don't like what you see, reshoot. You don't have to set up a screen to show the tape either, because you've already got a television set.

In many ways the video camera is actually beginning to replace the still camera. People who would never have thought of owning a movie camera are videotaping birthday parties, vacations, baby's first steps—a lot of things that would once have been the sole province of the still camera.

While it is not absolutely necessary to have a video camera when you're young in order to pursue a career in video later, many of the professionals that we talked to said that you should begin to familiarize yourself with the equipment as soon as you possibly can. We realize that video cameras, while cheaper than ever before, are still expensive. That's one of the reasons that we suggest that you join an audio-visual (AV) club at school, take a video course, or volunteer at a local cable station. You might also think of renting equipment to see if you like using it. In the New York area, video cameras rent for about twenty-five dollars a day, or seventy-five dollars for four days, still a high price.

Even if you have a camera, don't think that you will be able to turn out professional quality video. We once had a crew from CBS doing some taping in our house. There were half a dozen technicians and hundreds of thousands of dollars' worth of cameras, lighting equip-

Home video cameras are becoming smaller, cheaper, and easier to use.

ment, and all sorts of other gear. It took seven hours to shoot a segment that ultimately ran about six minutes. And this, we were told, was a fairly simple, trouble-free, and inexpensive assignment.

But Jerry Kramer, the director of "The Making of Thriller," told us that you can make a good video at any level. The most important thing is not your equipment, but your ideas—the thought that goes into making the tape. Not only will you gain experience in making videos, but you will have samples of your work to show to schools or prospective employers, just as a graphic artist has samples of his or her work in a portfolio.

Anybody can point a camera and press a button and take a picture, but to make a video takes planning. Let's take an example of a family celebration, like your kid sister's birthday party. Most people would just shoot a scene of blowing out the candles, cutting the cake, opening the presents, and perhaps a couple of games. The result would be a series of unrelated scenes—fine for memories and showing to the grandparents, but that's about it.

To make a video of the same event you would have to plan the concept, not just stand around and take the obvious shots. You might start by showing the family at breakfast in the morning. You could create a display of old photographs, featuring baby pictures of your sister and previous birthday parties. Then show preparations for the party and the high points of the party itself, which is all that most people usually shoot. You might wind up with the aftermath—your exhausted parents cleaning up the mess that is left.

This, of course, is an outline for a very simple video. But once you start planning shots and scenes, you are beginning to think like a director. You will begin to get a feel for what works and what doesn't.

If you become fairly proficient at shooting videos and you have, or have access to, editing equipment, you might even be able to make some money with your video camera. Other people might like to have birthday parties, anniversaries, weddings, and other major family events recorded on tape, and they won't have the equipment or skill to do the job.

Professional taping services are available, but not in every area, and they are expensive. Professional taping of a wedding can cost between seven hundred dollars and seventeen hundred dollars. You can beat that price. One strong word of warning—if you're going into videotaping as a business, be sure that you know what you're doing. If you undertake to videotape the wedding of your neighbor's daughter and half the tape turns up blank, you are not going to be able to reshoot. You will be embarrassed, and your neighbor will probably be furious.

There are more ambitious video projects that could gain you experience and recognition, if not money. You could tape school plays or sporting events. Video has penetrated most school systems, and some are quite sophisticated in the use of the equipment. But in many schools, use of video remains at a primitive level. The teacher sets up the camera, presses the button, and hopes that it all comes out. Sometimes it does, sometimes it doesn't. Even when it does, the tape doesn't look or sound very good. Offer your services, your expertise. You may actually know more about using the equipment than anyone else around.

Videotaped school events might be shown on local access channels. Your sister's birthday party would not be widely watched outside your own family, but the Little League game of the week might—it's the sort of event access coordinators like.

With a video camera you can make your own "movie" a lot more cheaply and easily than you could with conventional film. Again, the key to success with such a project is advance planning—know what you're going

Preparing to shoot a music video featuring the performance of a local band

to do—don't just stand out there with the camera while your friends run around screaming and making faces.

You can do music videos—not just shots of the band from different angles, but mixing the music with different images.

In order to do the more ambitious projects you would have to take some video courses, either in school—if they happen to be offered in your high school—in summer school at a community college, from the local access channel, or anywhere else you can find them. It would also be a good idea to keep up with articles in the video magazines on new techniques and developments.

With video increasingly being regarded as another medium for the artist, there are exhibitions and prizes for videos made by amateurs, just as there are exhibitions and prizes for amateur painters and sculptors. Your own videos might also help you get into video programs in college and give you a shot at scholarship and grant money as well.

What you do now can give you a big head start in your future career.

CHAPTER SIX
VIDEO EVERYWHERE

Video is becoming something we use all the time and take for granted. We may not be fully aware of how important it has become. Because video is so much cheaper and easier to use than film, and more versatile and dynamic than still photography, it's replacing or augmenting film and photography in many fields. And it's a trend with no end in sight. All of this means video training will be very important in a huge number of jobs in the future—jobs outside of the traditional television studio.

Who uses video? Well, to begin with, museums, like the famous Smithsonian Institution in Washington, D.C., rely on video both behind the scenes and for displays. Folklorists and historians use video when interviewing. It's an effective way to record vanishing ways of life and preserve a picture of the past. Video is used in documentation for insurance policies and is part of the process of patenting an invention. You'll find video on archaeological sites and in apartment and home security systems. It's a key element in training athletes. Video may be the referee of the future. Even today sports events are videotaped, and woe to the official who makes a bad call because the call is on record.

There are videotape catalogues and brochures demonstrating products consumers can order by mail. Every major racetrack has its own television system to show when the horses cross the finish line. The studio of a creative artist is no longer necessarily simply a room with a skylight, an easel, and paints. Many avant-garde artists work in audio-video media—art forms for the space age.

Video cameras go down oil wells. Politicians use video. Companies in just about every industry you can think of run media centers to store, buy, and produce videotapes. Most companies use video in training programs where videocassettes are the means of giving product information, teaching new sales techniques, providing information about on-the-job safety measures, and showing production-line workers how to do a particular job.

Video is also widely used for employee-orientation sessions. Many large corporations use video for their annual stockholders' reports and even have video newsletters. Video in corporate communications involves making public and community relations videotapes and preparing and presenting video product displays.

One recent college graduate who loves to travel took a job with a company that makes school furniture. She attends conventions of school administrators from Maine to Hawaii, showing videotapes of furniture made by the company she works for. Even in jobs where other things count more than video, video still has its place. Another recent graduate, a proficient skier, went to work as an assistant manager at a ski resort. High on the list of job requirements was running a video camera and knowing how to edit videotape.

There are companies concerned solely or primarily with video production. They provide the facilities and expertise to individuals and organizations that need video. Production includes video resumes, industrial video documentaries, sales training videos, instructional tapes, commercials, video for fashion shows, for new services, art exhibits, audio-visual shows, and promotions. Video production companies provide studio space, cameras, lights, microphones, editing services, and personnel to run the equipment. Studio space is rented out for theatrical readings, auditions, workshops, and screenings. Clients are performers like opera singers, actors, and dancers, but major corporations like IBM also use the services of companies that specialize in video, as do casting directors, public relations firms, marketing firms, surgeons, lawyers, architects, real estate agencies, beauty salons—just about any business you can think of. There are even multicultural, multilingual video production companies, experts in dubbing who adapt and supervise scripts and provide technical direction for translating on-the-air programming into foreign languages.

Video is an important part of the advertising industry. Agencies hire media directors and buyers who purchase television airtime for spot announcements and decide which TV programs clients should sponsor. Account executives who supervise advertising campaigns must understand all advertising media, including television, while copywriters have the job of writing copy for TV commercials and that means everything from announcements to voice-overs and dialogue.

Video has spawned trade magazines, which are publications targeted at people working within the television-cable-video industry. There are also popular consumer-oriented magazines like *Video* and *Video Review* which run articles on the latest developments in equipment, reviews of television programs, information about which films are available on cassette, and other news of interest to video buffs. Both trade and consumer magazines hire editors, writers, and photographers.

And don't forget the thousands of retail stores devoted to video, and that means work for store owners, managers, and salespeople. Many such stores sell or rent cassettes of movies which you can watch at home on your television set if you have a VCR. Other stores sell mainly consumer electronic equipment like VCRs and video cameras.

You may already have come across one new use of video—the production of video yearbooks. Like the regular printed high school yearbook, video yearbooks cover drama club plays, the homecoming game, awards presentations, and the senior prom. Because they don't have to be sent off to the printer, video yearbooks have one big advantage over conventional yearbooks—they can include the entire year's activities right through graduation itself. And for an extra fee students can purchase personalized videotapes which may include an interview at the senior prom or capture the moment they're handed their diploma. The audio side of the yearbook is special, too. The sound is strictly rock, featuring the hit songs of the year, plus the prom theme song.

Almost every school system, college, and university uses video, so if you plan to teach, you might explore video education. You couldn't have made it as far as high school without seeing at least some television shows in your classroom. Usually these are broadcast by public television channels and are basically educational in content. Some schools really go all out for television with various sorts of coordinators and AV instructors or media arts teachers.

Besides instructing students, people working in video in school systems often instruct teachers in the use of video as an educational tool and keep up with the latest programming and technological developments in video. If colleges provide courses on film, video, telecommunications, broadcast journalism, and television-oriented performing arts, then they must employ people to teach them.

Many large colleges have closed-circuit TV linking up separate buildings and different departments and classrooms. Much of the programming shown is created right on campus in the school's television studios. Some schools have full-time directors who oversee the operation of the college television facilities. At really big schools, besides a director there may be a whole staff, including engineers who run the closed-circuit TV system.

At the college level you'll find people in charge of selecting and purchasing equipment from cassettes all the way up to state-of-the-art electronic learning laboratories. You'll find media librarians in charge of the circulation of video-cassettes and the building of videotape collections. They're highly knowledgeable about what's available on cassette. Some colleges have special video instructors teaching in the department of education. These instructors have to know as much about education as video. And, of course, every school has to have somebody to maintain and repair video equipment.

Hospitals also use video extensively. Let's take a look at one, the famous Johns Hopkins Medical Center in Baltimore, Maryland. In 1947 the closed-circuit televising of a meeting took place at Johns Hopkins, making it the first medical institution to use TV.

At the Children's Center of Johns Hopkins Medical Center, young patients are often featured in shows produced by the center.

The medical center uses video in a variety of ways. Patients are entertained by watching movies on a closed-circuit TV system. They also watch shows developed for patient education. There's a separate channel for children's television. But children who are patients at Johns Hopkins get to do more than watch. The kids actually star in shows they make themselves and even do the camera work, helped by an adult who is the special coordinator of children's programs at the hospital.

Video programs are also produced for training doctors in surgical, medical, and health-related areas. Some of the programs taped are then marketed.

Then there's microwave TV, allowing two-way audio and one-way video communication between Johns Hopkins and other medical institutions. Live lectures can therefore be broadcast from Johns Hopkins to students training at other hospitals. Another aspect of video production at Johns Hopkins is to coordinate satellite TV broadcasting or reception. This job requires first-rate organizing skills. A coordinator must rent a portable earth station, have it delivered, get telephones installed, and cope with organizing a program that would link people in different parts of the country or, ultimately, the world.

For a job in video at Johns Hopkins you must have a masters degree in communications or a related field. Some knowledge of medical terminology and anatomy is helpful. You have to be a good camera operator, be able to write scripts, direct, and edit. Theatrical experience helps, too—you often wind up making sets. And you should know community resources.

At the moment it isn't easy to find video-related jobs in the medical field but this will almost certainly change. With a minimum of equipment small hospitals could put together innovative video programs for much less than the cost of prepackaged health-related programs. So as video becomes more and more a part of everyday life, hospital jobs should open up.

Another big user of video—probably the biggest—is the government. It may surprise you to learn that when it comes to the production of visual media, Hollywood isn't in the same class with Washington. And the government now produces far more video than film.

The federal government uses the most. The largest federal agencies operate their own video production units, with people working in production, engineering, and most of the areas you'd find in commercial TV.

All levels of government use video in training employees and for public information programs. The Department of Agriculture alone produces an enormous number of videos on everything from health-related subjects to farming techniques. At the state level, public health, youth services, law enforcement, agriculture, and transportation are important agencies when it comes to the use of video.

Because of the size and scope of its video production, let's look more closely at one particular federal government agency, the Department of Agriculture. Television is used extensively to inform the public about agency programs, policies, research results, and activities. Television programming is provided to local channels in farm areas in two ways, via satellite and on video cassettes.

In addition to regular services, news conferences held by the secretary of agriculture are fed live to stations by satellite. There are also special TV satellite events featuring the secretary of agriculture and guests. Farm broadcasters at stations throughout the country phone in questions to the secretary and/or guests who answer the questions on camera.

Regular USDA video programming includes farm shows, programs for consumers, and general news and commentary. For example, "A Better Way" is a

The Department of Agriculture produces a variety of shows aimed specifically at farmers.

half-hour weekly show with topics ranging from nutrition, money-saving ideas, and environmental issues, to home-improvement tips. "Down to Earth" is a short news show. There are even shorter news features, about a minute and a half, produced on location, which are mailed to stations on request. Subjects cover agricultural research and marketing, rural development, consumer interests, forestry, and conservation.

The department produces regular news updates on farm production programs, export news, and production outlooks as well as TV service announcements, mostly on food safety and nutrition.

Ordinarily, to work for the government you must receive a career civil service appointment. You'll need a bachelor's degree or comparable experience to qualify in video. There are certain forms you must fill out and procedures to follow. Competition is keen. But when the time comes to start job hunting, check and see if a government job is for you. If it is, you might have a shot at doing a lot of work in video.

While we're on the subject of jobs, here's a random sample of job openings, the sort you'd hear about through a college placement service.

> Creative Writer/Producer wanted to write and produce local TV commercials. Bachelor's degree and strong communication skills required.

> Video technician for component level maintenance work with ¾ VCR, single and 3-tube cameras commercial insertion equipment, and fully equipped remote unit.

> Account Executive/TV Sales to service and sell marketing concepts to existing and new advertisers. Emphasis on extensive media research, TV broadcast sales.

Maybe you'd be interested in applying as a

> Teleconference Development specialist to train and direct university faculty in satellite teleconferencing. Will be responsible for writing and directing programs and producing TV tape segments for regular TV broadcasts.
>
> Director, university information services, comprehensive public relations program. Must prepare and edit press releases, speeches, and develop radio and TV programming.
>
> Art Director, experience in video/film medical illustration.

Maybe this would be for you.

> Senior Producer—experience in any of the following: production, reporting, on-camera talent, directing. Experience in performing arts or public TV preferred. Responsible for content, planning, assembling, and producing and/or directing TV programs in broad area of visual and performing arts.

Chances are you're not ready to make decisions yet. And there may be new types of jobs by the time you're ready that we don't even know about yet. But it might not be a bad idea to at least give the whole subject a little thought now, to make everything easier in the future.

CHAPTER SEVEN

EDUCATION IN VIDEO

What's the best way to break into a career in video? Most experts will tell you college is the surest route. Nobody sums it up better than Jerry Kramer, who's produced several successful David Lee Roth music videos and who directed "The Making of Thriller." "If you're really interested in this field, the thing to do is to go to college and study film or video. You'll get hands-on experience. You'll gain technical advantages. You'll engage in creative discussion with your peers. College is also for having fun, for maturing."

Granted, some technical jobs don't require a degree, for example, videotape engineers, audio-video engineers, or lighting directors. But often these jobs do require some form of technical training and licensing. Besides, don't kid yourself, most jobs at the decision-making level go to people who have college degrees and in some cases, advanced degrees. Forget the exceptions, the maverick geniuses who make it to the top by breaking all the rules. Though it would be wonderful if something so exciting happened to you, you shouldn't count on it. No matter how talented you are, you just might not be that lucky.

If you're aiming at becoming a program director, a sales manager, a chief engineer, a graphic artist, a director, producer, production manager, even a performer who works in front of the camera, you will need a college education. Five or ten years down the line college will be even more important than it is now. Look at broadcast networks today. You need a college degree just to start as a page or in security at CBS. By and large cable channels are more flexible, but that's only because cable is newer. Systems and organizations tend to become more rigid and bureaucratic as time passes, so as more and more people go to work in cable you can be assured that job standards and educational qualifications will become tougher and tighter.

If you don't want, or can't afford, four full years of college, there are schools, like Pasadena City College in California, and the University of Cincinnati in Ohio, that offer a two-year program in video. Check out colleges in the region where you live, including community colleges, to see what video courses are offered. Don't neglect continuing education courses and evening classes. There are also trade schools that provide mini-courses or short-term training programs, especially in technical areas. You must make sure, though, that the trade school you're interested in is solidly established and has a good job placement record.

But since, even if you're a whiz with a camera, a college degree can only help, we'll assume that's where you're headed. If your talents are in areas requiring strong verbal skills, then college is definitely for you, since words will be the tools of your trade. Look upon college as an opportunity, a foot in the door, a way of meeting professors who will guide you in career choices, a place to learn where the growth areas of video are, and where the exciting jobs will be in the future. College will give you access to internships and a school-run job placement service.

If you're not prepared to commit yourself to film school (video and film are often related subjects at college), relax, there are alternatives. You may prefer to study acting, communications, management, business, or pursue a liberal arts curriculum. You can still explore video through extracurricular activities. Working in your college television studio in your spare time is wonderful hands-on training. Experiment, take your time, explore different aspects of education. You may not want to specialize till later in college or graduate school.

Film and video director Michael Collins points out that, while education at film school is very useful, "it's also possible for one to become a director if one is an actor, an editor, or a scriptwriter. Camera people become directors. Choreographers are well situated to direct music videos. College mainly gives you a community of interest. But experience is wonderful training, too. Travel, live!"

So don't feel you must begin college with your future all mapped out. Still, if video is a central interest, you'll take it into account when choosing a college. And there are schools strong in video in every part of the country. New York University and the University of California at Los Angeles are noted for film studies. UCLA's Motion Picture/Television Division has one of the largest noncommercial film and video facilities in America, plus a vast archive of telefilms and videotapes. Major studios, networks, and production companies regularly shoot feature films, commercials, and television series on campus. According to Steve Moore of UCLA's video department, students at UCLA are encouraged to become independent video producers. "They shoot weddings, that kind of thing." This is also a great way to earn extra money while you're at school.

The School of Telecommunications at Ohio University in Athens, Ohio, offers a bachelor's degree in video production and is one of the few schools in the country to screen nominees for national awards for local television programs. The University of Wisconsin has courses in cable television. At the graduate level, the University of Texas offers an advanced course on cable franchising. The radio-TV department at the University of North Carolina at Chapel Hill includes cable TV studies in its broadcast curriculum.

Though you'll want to weigh many factors when it comes to picking a college, a good way to learn about courses in video is to ask a school to send you a course catalogue. Read it carefully. You might want to talk to your guidance counselor at high school and see if he or she recommends any particular school. A visit to see its video facilities is a good idea, and you don't have to wait until you're a junior or senior to do this.

Despite the many good colleges throughout the country, we have chosen to focus on two just to give you an idea of the kind of training available. Both schools have outstanding video programs. The first is Syracuse University in Syracuse, New York, home of the S. I. Newhouse School of Public Communications. Syracuse was a pioneer in cable, offering courses in it before most colleges began taking cable seriously. The other school is Emerson College in Boston, Massachusetts, a school devoted solely to communication arts and sciences.

Students in the broadcast journalism program at the Newhouse School prepare a half-hour news broadcast every day which is aired on the university's closed-cir-

A student edits his experimental video production at the College of Visual and Performing Arts, Syracuse University.

A student producer editing a tape at the College of Visual and Performing Arts, Syracuse

cuit television station. This kind of training is especially important because news is such a major part of local and cable programming, and can only be produced locally. So a lot of the jobs available in television are in news.

Up-to-date equipment is a vital part of video training, and at Syracuse an entire facility, Newhouse II, part of the Newhouse Communications Center, is devoted primarily to telecommunications and film. It's loaded with the latest television equipment.

Newhouse telecommunications programs deal with television, radio, film, and allied technologies. Students can specialize in telecommunications management with an emphasis on television programming. They can work towards a Bachelor of Science degree in producing for electronic media. Skills are developed in video and audio production, television studio operations, graphics, and production of film for television.

Would-be scriptwriters take courses focusing on writing in telecommunications. Camera work, scripting, editing, and criticism are part of the film sequence. Public relations students learn to make audio-visual presentations.

Syracuse's School of Visual and Performing Arts offers courses in advertising design, with a heavy emphasis on conceptual problem solving in television, as part of the Department of Visual Communication. Art education students can take courses preparing them for careers in educational television. Computer graphics is another program of study relying heavily on videotape. Computer graphics are used to create special effects in film and are used widely in television newsrooms.

In addition to a full film program with courses in video, students may, if they wish, explore video research, a highly experimental program in which the video screen takes the place of the artist's canvas. A tape made by Syracuse video research students won an Ace Award for cable excellence and was shown on cable in California and Manhattan. Drama students at Syracuse can get a Bachelor of Fine Arts degree in film with either an art or drama emphasis.

Stimulating is the best way to describe Emerson College's Emerson Independent Video (EIV), a closed-circuit production company which has produced shows for local television stations and Warner Cable. Television students at Emerson prepare for careers in network, local, cable, and pay television, as well as in corporate, educational, and independent video production. Students from the theater arts division perform before the television camera in productions sponsored jointly with the division of mass communications. In the journalism division of Emerson College, courses are taught in news analysis for television and television news production. There is a strong film program as well. Television production courses are taught by established professionals like Marsha Della-Guistina, professor of journalism, who recently won an Emmy Award for television news production.

Students concentrating on television at Emerson work on news features, music videos, documentaries, and public service announcements. Emerson stresses an interdisciplinary approach, and students from many departments can take a number of unusual courses. The school also emphasizes a hands-on, rather than a theoretical, approach. One particular children's television course allows students to review the content and production approaches of major children's television programs such as "Sesame Street," "Mister Rogers' Neighborhood," and "Nickelodeon," the cable TV network for children. A course in the art of makeup for television is taught. The Department of Writing, Literature and Publishing offers a course in audio-visual project development, where students complete a full-length

*Professional video facility in the
Newhouse School, Syracuse University*

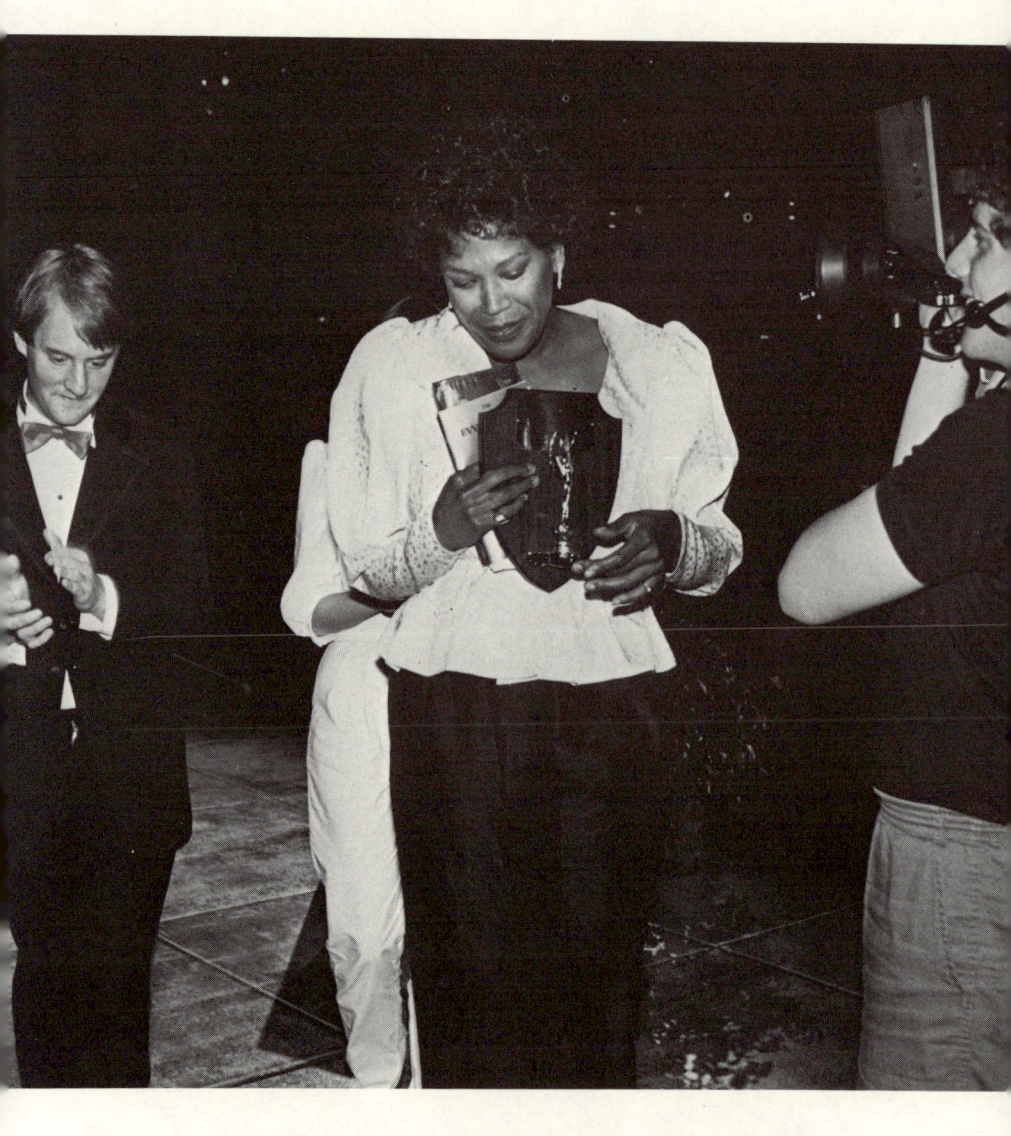

Each year Emerson College students produce the EVVY Awards, modeled after the EMMY Awards. Shown here is Boston TV anchor Liz Walker, WBZ-TV, receiving an EVVY award.

film or television script for a documentary or educational or business-related topic. The department also offers a course in writing comedy, which allows students to write television situation-comedy scripts. Writing is an important and sometimes overlooked area in television.

Students at Emerson practice being a television interviewer. The continuing-education division offers a course on women and broadcast management. Emerson students learn how to set up a corporate media department and prepare audio-visual materials. They also find out how to write television spot commercials. Emerson students are encouraged to be versatile.

But there is a part of your education as important as classes and study sessions in the library. Emerson, Syracuse, and many other schools offer students internships. For hands-on experience internships can't be beat. Internships take you a step beyond college, giving you professional experience. Basically, an internship is a period of time, possibly three months or so, spent working within a corporation or at a television channel. Usually, you receive no pay but can get college credit. Major broadcast networks always give credit. Interns often work as many as three full days a week at their internships, so a student gets a realistic and intensive view of what the field is like. Remember, no matter how good a school is, it's still a protected environment. Things will be done differently on the job.

To producer Tamara Wells, "the most important training you get in college is an internship. I got my first job at the company where I was an intern and worked my way into free-lancing."

And many a local cable channel executive will tell you they would always hire someone with hands-on experience over someone without. Cable interns get immediate firsthand knowledge of a cable system and the exposure to what it's like on a day-by-day basis, so they can decide whether working in cable is really for them.

Benefiting from its Boston location, Emerson interns work for a broad range of employers. They've been news assistants at ABC-TV and the Cable News Network. They've interned in public relations at Columbia Pictures, and in promotion at Capital Records. At Syracuse, internships in advertising, local cable TV, and with major broadcast networks are an important part of the Newhouse School program. The casting department of NBC's "As the World Turns" recently contacted Syracuse asking for a student to intern as an assistant in the casting department.

One alternative to college is the military. You can get solid video training there. You might decide to remain in the service, continuing your work in video, or you might decide to use the training you receive there to prepare for a civilian job. Let's take the Air Force as an example. All the audio-visual skills are taught somewhere in the Air Force. Air Force AV facilities train personnel enlisted in the Army, Navy, and Marines as well. A thorough and intensive course in journalism and broadcasting is one of several available educational programs, and a vast amount of on-the-job training is also provided. The truly talented may receive further specialized training. And if you stick with it, there are plenty of opportunities for travel since many of the military facilities are overseas.

Scenes from experimental videos created by students at the College of Visual and Performing Arts, Syracuse University

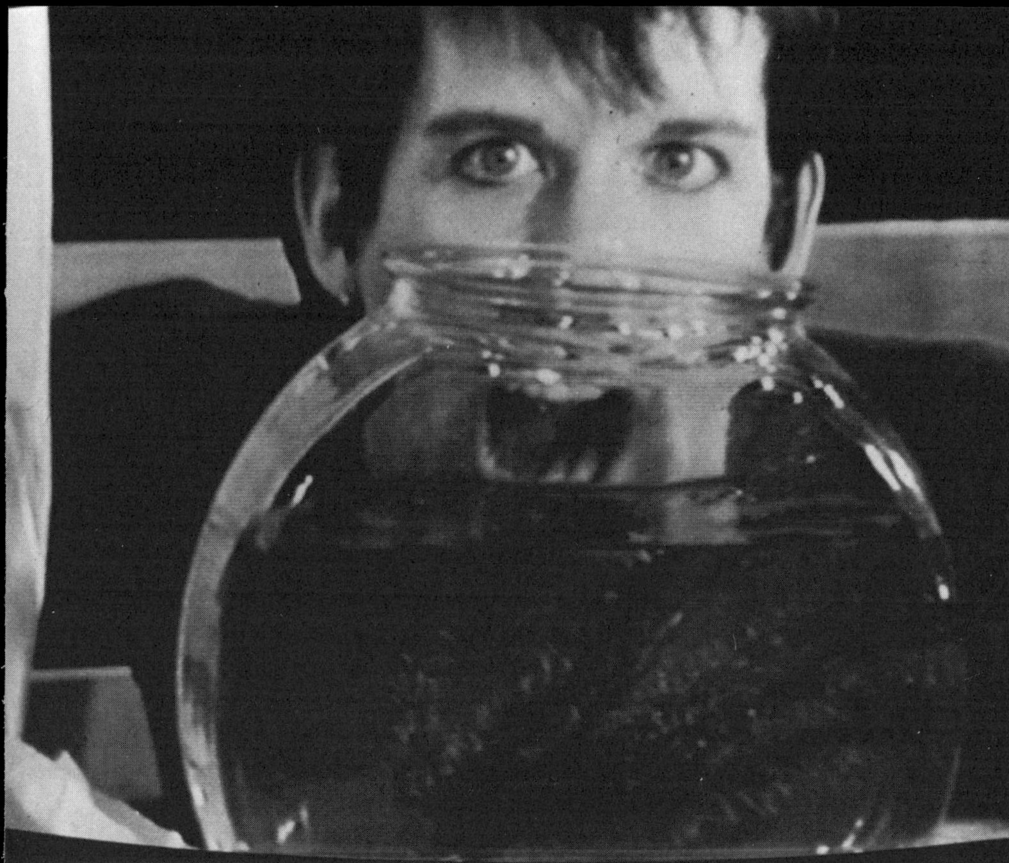

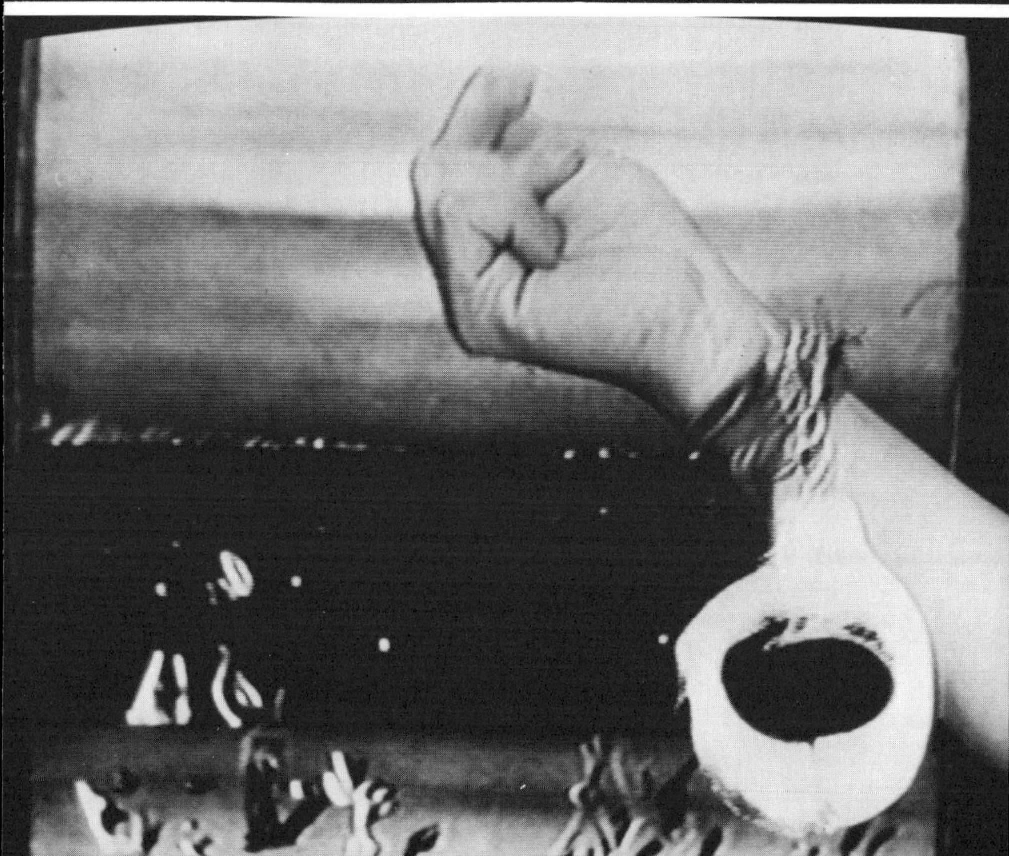

The best way to find out about service-oriented video programs is to get in touch with a local recruiter. In the Air Force, enlistees take a qualifying (SAT-like) test. Depending on the score, the recruiter will go over the type of options open to you and whether you should focus on electronics or areas requiring verbal skills. Whatever training you're eligible for, you may even be able to go on delayed enlistment if all video jobs are filled at the time you apply. A background in math and electronics is useful, so bear that in mind when planning high school courses and extracurricular activities.

But why wait until you're through with high school to become involved in video? Contact your local cable channel right now and ask to work as a volunteer. New York State has a summer school of the arts which includes experimenting with video. Get in touch with your high school guidance department, your art or media arts teacher, or write to your state board of education and find out if there's something similar where you live. Find out if a nearby community center or college has any after-school or summer programs in video for high school students.

Join your high school AV club. You'll tape sports events, plays, and special classroom programs. There are schools where AV club members do news broadcasts and present other programs on the local cable access channel. Some schools have media arts courses where you get school credits. There is also the photography club. The still photographer and the video camera operator both see the world through the lens of their camera.

If you're interested in working in front of the camera, then join the high school drama club, chorus, debating club, or participate in any extracurricular activity that will get you used to performing in public. To sharpen interviewing techniques become a reporter on the high school newspaper. Write for the paper if you think you want to be a scriptwriter someday. Write for the literary magazine at your school, too. There are more jobs in video requiring writing skills than you may imagine. But most of all, keep making videos.

Ask Jerry Kramer. He'll tell you. "The main thing is to keep making videos, super 8, or quarter-inch. This will give you most of the benefits of realizing a vision and lets you see whether you got what you wanted. You learn from every job and experience. The most important point is that you had a good idea. You can make wonderful videos at any technological level and people look for creativity. So a good video at any level can further your career."

Follow this advice and by the time you get to college you'll already be well on your way to a future in video.

CHAPTER EIGHT

WHERE TO GO FROM HERE

PERIODICALS

Remember, the related fields of television cable and video are changing all the time, in regard to technology, employment, economics, laws, and just about everything. These changes are chronicled in a huge variety of publications that are read avidly by those working in the field. Listed below are some of the best-known publications. They cover many different areas and no single publication will be of interest to everyone. The actor trying to land a part in a new soap opera will read *Variety,* but will find nothing of use in *CableVision.* A cable systems manager might find dipping into *Variety* amusing, but for information that will help her in her work she'll turn to *CableVision.*

Some, but not many, of the publications are available on the newsstand. More may be found in a well-stocked public library or a college library. If you are on good terms with the staff at the local cable channel or broadcast channel, you might get a look at some of the publications they get. If all else fails, write the publisher and see if you can get a single copy. The subscription price for most of these publications is very steep so don't even think of subscribing until you get a good look at a couple of issues and decide if the publication will really be useful to you.

Backstage. 330 W. 42nd St., New York, NY 10036. A weekly for the communications/entertainment industry with emphasis on behind-the-scenes personnel.

Broadcasting. 1735 De Sales St. NW, Washington, DC 20036. A comprehensive weekly on all aspects of broadcasting including cable TV.

Broadcasting Cablecasting Sourcebook. 1735 De Sales St. NW, Washington, DC 20036. An annual directory by the publishers of *Broadcasting* of all the cable systems, suppliers, etc.

CableVision. 2500 Curtis St., Suite 200, Denver, CO 80205. A weekly newsmagazine of the cable industry.

Daily Variety. 1400 N. Cahuenga Blvd., Hollywood, CA 90028. The daily newspaper of the entertainment industry.

Filmmakers Monthly. P.O. Box 115, Ward Hill, MA 08130. Not just for filmmakers but for independent video producers as well.

The Hollywood Reporter. 6715 Sunset Blvd., Hollywood, CA 90028. A daily covering the entertainment industry.

Home Video. 474 Park Ave., S., New York, NY 10016. A monthly on the home entertainment industry.

Millimeter. 12 E. 46th St., New York, NY 10017. A monthly on film, television, cable, etc. Emphasis on work behind the camera.

Multi-Channel News. 300 S. Jackson St., Denver, CO 80209. A weekly on the cable industry with an excellent help-wanted section.

Variety. 154 W. 46th St., New York, NY 10036. The weekly bible of the entertainment industry. Contains information on the cable industry.

Video. 460 W. 34th St., New York, NY 10001.

Video Review. 359 E. 81st St., New York, NY 10028. Two publications for the home video buff with lots of information on new cameras and other equipment.

BOOKS

Writing about television cable and video is practically an industry in itself. Below is a representative selection of books about various aspects of the field that you may find useful and interesting. Some of the books, particularly those dealing with jobs and equipment, may be updated regularly. Always try to get the latest edition.

Brenner, Alfred. *TV Scriptwriter's Handbook.* Cincinnati: Writers Digest Books, 1980. Tips on writing for television.

Bretz, Rudy. *Handbook for Producing Educational and Public Access Programs for Cable Television.* Englewood Cliffs, NJ: Educational Technology Publications, 1976. Though dated, can still be useful in high schools with television classes.

Cohen, Daniel and Susan. *The Kid's Guide to Home Video.* New York: Archway, 1984. The authors of this book look at cable TV, the VCR, and other changes in video technology. For young readers.

Cohen, Henry B., and Apar, Bruce. *The Home Video Book.* New York: Watson-Guptill/Amphoto, 1981.

———. *The Home Video Survival Guide.* New York: Watson-Guptill/Amphoto, 1983. Books for the serious home video buff.

David, Ed. *The Intelligent Idiot's Guide to Home Video Equipment.* Philadelphia: Running Press, 1983. Certainly not for idiots, but a relatively simple guide to an increasingly complicated field.

Denny, Jon S. *Careers in Cable TV.* New York: Barnes and Noble, 1983. Brightly written, interesting, and extremely useful. A must.

Ellis, Elmo I. *Opportunities in Broadcasting.* Skokie, IL: VCM Career Horizons, 1982. Covers radio as well as broadcast television.

Hollingsworth, T. R. *Tune in to a Television Career.* New York: Julian Messner, 1984. The focus is on broadcast television. For junior high and high school readers.

National Cable Television Association. *Careers in Cable.* Washington, DC, 1983. Only a thirty-page pamphlet, but packed with helpful information.

National Video Clearinghouse. *The Video Sourcebook.* 3rd ed., Syosset, NY, 1982. Where to find the video information and/or equipment that you need.

Rather, Dan, with Herskowitz, Mickey. *The Camera Never Blinks.* New York: Morrow, 1977. Observations of television's number one anchorperson.

Reed, Maxine K. and Robert M. *Career Opportunities in Television and Video.* New York: Facts on File, 1982. The most complete rundown available on specific jobs. A must for the novice job seeker.

Roman, James W. *Cablemania.* Englewood Cliffs, NJ: Prentice-Hall, 1983. The cable industry and how it grew.

Sandler, Bernard. *In Front of the Camera.* New York: Dutton, 1981. Advice on how to look good on TV.

Sapan, Joshua. *Making It in Cable TV.* New York: Perigee Books, 1984. Excellent listing of specific job opportunities.

Savitch, Jessica. *Anchorwoman.* New York: Putnam, 1982. The TV anchor desk is not just for men.

Television Digest. *The Television Factbook.* Washington, DC. Updated annually. Packed with statistics, names, addresses, etc. A bible of the television industry. There is also cable addenda to the book.

COLLEGES

If you're college bound, here's a list of schools strong in either journalism and communications and/or film and video. Many are also strong in one or another aspect of the performing arts. The list will help you get started on your search for the right school but it is far from complete. There are just too many good schools. If we listed them all, there wouldn't be any room in this book to tell you about anything else.

Because the colleges on this list have varied programs and specializations, you'll have to check further to find out which ones are for you. Since we felt it was important to include colleges from every region, we can't promise that all are equally good. But it wouldn't help you much to learn only about schools you couldn't go to. Sure, UCLA and NYU have dazzling film and video departments, but if you're a midwesterner planning to go to college in the Midwest, so what?

Another factor in our listing of schools is cost. Though we've included private colleges, we've made sure that plenty of state schools are listed. Tuition is much lower at state schools, especially for in-state residents, than at private colleges. But don't forget to find out about colleges near you offering two-year programs in video. Most metropolitan areas have fine colleges that serve mainly commuters who live at home.

To find out what a school offers, write for information. You can also go to the library and read about the school in a guide to colleges. Don't be shy about asking your guidance counselor to help you. After all, choosing a school is a major decision.

ALABAMA

University of Alabama
Department of Broadcast and Film Communication
PO Box D
University, AL 35486

CALIFORNIA

University of California, Los Angeles (UCLA)
Theater Arts Department
405 Hilgard Ave.
Los Angeles, CA 90024

University of Southern California
Annenberg School of Communications
University Park
Los Angeles, CA 90024

FLORIDA

University of Florida
Broadcasting Department
315 Stadium Building
Gainesville, FL 32611

GEORGIA

University of Georgia
Radio-TV-Film Department
School of Journalism
Athens, GA 30602

ILLINOIS

Northwestern University
Radio-Television and Film Department
School of Speech
Evanston, IL 60201

INDIANA

Indiana University
Telecommunications Department
Radio and Television Center
College of Arts and Sciences
Bloomington, IN 47401

IOWA

Drake University
Radio-Television Department
25th and University
Des Moines, IA 50311

KANSAS

University of Kansas
Radio-Television-Film Department
217 Flint Hall
Lawrence, KS 66045

MARYLAND

University of Maryland
Radio-Television-Film Division
College Park, MD 20742

MASSACHUSETTS

Emerson College
Mass Communications Department
148 Beacon St.
Boston, MA 02116

MICHIGAN

Michigan State University
Telecommunications Department
East Lansing, MI 48824

University of Michigan
Speech Communication and Theatre Department
2020 Frieze Building
Ann Arbor, MI 48109

MINNESOTA

University of Minnesota, Minneapolis/St. Paul
Speech-Communications Department
Folwell Hall
Minneapolis, MN 55455

MISSOURI

University of Missouri, Columbia
Division of Radio-Television-Film
Speech and Dramatic Art Department
200 Swallow Hall
Columbia, MO 65201

MONTANA

University of Montana
Radio-Television Department
School of Journalism
Missoula, MT 59801

NEBRASKA

University of Nebraska
Television-Radio-Film Department
Lincoln, NE 68508

NEVADA

University of Nevada, Las Vegas
School of Journalism
4505 Maryland Parkway
Las Vegas, NV 89154

NEW YORK

Ithaca College
Department of Television-Radio
School of Communications
Danby Rd.
Ithaca, NY 14850

New York University (NYU)
Undergraduate Institute of Film and Television
Tisch School of the Arts
51 W. 4th St.
New York, NY 10003

Syracuse University
Telecommunications/Film Department
S. I. Newhouse School of Public Communications
215 University Place
Syracuse, NY 13210

NORTH CAROLINA

University of North Carolina at Chapel Hill
Department of Radio, Television, and Motion Pictures
College of Arts and Sciences
Swain Hall 044A
Chapel Hill, NC 27514

OHIO

Ohio University
Radio-Television Department, College of Fine Arts
Athens, OH 45701

OKLAHOMA

Oral Roberts University
Communication Arts Department
7777 South Lewis
Tulsa, OK 74171

OREGON

University of Oregon
Telecommunications Area
Department of Speech
Villard Hall
Eugene, OR 97403

PENNSYLVANIA

Temple University
Department of Radio-Television-Film
School of Communications and Theater
Broad and Montgomery Sts.
Philadelphia, PA 19122

University of Pennsylvania
Annenberg School of Communications
3620 Walnut St.
Philadelphia, PA 19104

SOUTH CAROLINA

University of South Carolina
Media Arts Department
Columbia, SC 29208

TEXAS

Baylor University
Division of Radio-Television-Film
Waco, TX 76706

University of Texas at Austin
Department of Radio-Television-Film
School of Communications
Austin, TX 78712

VIRGINIA

James Madison University
Communication Arts Department
Harrisonburg, VA 22801

WASHINGTON

Washington State University
Communications Department
Pullman, WA 99163

WISCONSIN

University of Wisconsin, Madison
Department of Communication Arts
Vilas Communication Hall
821 University Ave.
Madison, WI 53201

INTERNSHIPS, SCHOLARSHIPS, AND GRANTS

Because internships, apprenticeships, and training programs are so vital to careers in video, you might want to start exploring these programs now. The following list will give you an idea of the kinds of internships available. Though there are some internships for high school students, far more are available for college students. Colleges often give you credit for an internship and sometimes the internship will even pay a modest stipend. But in terms of experience, an internship is worth gold.

We have also included a brief selection of scholarships and grants. Write to the organization offering the scholarship if you want to learn more. Your high school guidance counselor can help you find out about scholarships and, of course, you should always ask about financial aid when you apply to any college. Directories with information about scholarships and other forms of financial aid are available in libraries and bookstores.

Remember, while you're in high school you may be able to work as a volunteer at your local public television or cable TV channel. It's worth a phone call to find out. You can also contact local advertising agencies and see if they offer internships you could apply for.

INTERNSHIPS

American Advertising Federation
1225 Connecticut Ave. NW
Washington, DC 20036
Local internships in television advertising.

American Film Institute
2021 North Western Ave.
Beverly Hills, CA 90027
Internships in television news directing and film production.

Broadway/Hollywood Video Production
PO Box 1314
Englewood Cliffs, NJ 07632
Internships in video production.

Channel 12
Grassroots Television
Box 2006
Aspen, CO 81611
Internships in television production.

International Alliance of
Theatrical Stage Employees (IATSE)
1515 Broadway, Suite 601
New York, NY 10036
Apprenticeships in television art direction, makeup, costuming, and properties.

KATU-TV
Fisher Broadcasting, Inc.
2153 NE Sandy Blvd.
PO Box 8799
Portland, OR 97208
Internships in television operations, sales, public affairs, administration, news, programming, production.

KDUB-TV
One Dubuque Plaza
Dubuque, IA 52001
Internships in television news, production, and engineering.

Media Study/Buffalo
207 Delaware Ave.
Buffalo, NY 14202
High school internships in video.

WBAL-TV
3800 Hooper Ave.
Baltimore, MD 21211
Internships in television production.

WEAR-TV
Box 12278
Pensacola, FL 32581
Internships in television production and news.

WTOL-TV
Cosmos Broadcasting Corporation
PO Box 715
Toledo, OH 43695
Internships in television news.

SCHOLARSHIPS AND GRANTS

Corporation for Public Broadcasting
1111 16th St. NW
Washington, DC 20036

Grants to public television stations for use in training women and members of minority groups.

National Academy of Television Arts and Sciences
110 W. 57th St.
New York, NY 10019

Scholarship to ten schools to be awarded to outstanding students in communications.

Society of Motion Picture and Television Engineers
Scholarships and Grants
862 Scarsdale Ave.
Scarsdale, NY 10583

Scholarships for the undergraduate study of film and television technology and science.

University Film Association
Scholarship Awards Program
Department of Radio/TV/Film
University of Texas, Austin
Austin, TX 78712

Scholarships for film/video production and research.

ORGANIZATIONS

Most professional associations in the industry are only open to people already at work in the field. However, here are some that you might wish to contact.

Foundation for Community Service Cable TV
5616 Geary Blvd., Suite 212
San Francisco, CA 94121
415-387-0200

If you're interested in cable and live in California you should get in contact with this state-mandated foundation which encourages the use of access channels. It provides a packet of useful information for free.

National Cable Television Association
1724 Massachusetts Ave. NW
Washington, DC 20036
202-775-3550
This is the major trade association for the cable industry and from time to time NCTA issues publications of interest to those thinking of a career in cable.

National Federation of Local Cable Programmers
906 Pennsylvania Ave. SE
Washington, DC 20003
202-544-7272
If you're interested in access cable, NFLCP may be for you. It has a magazine and newsletter which cover the access scene throughout the country including listings of regional conferences and job opportunities.

Women in Cable
2033 M St. NW, Suite 703
Washington, DC 20036
202-296-4218
Publishes a newsletter and runs career seminars for women in the field.

CABLE NETWORKS

Some cable networks like HBO and MTV run twenty-four hours a day and are widely available. Others have limited programming and are available on only a small number of systems. What follows is a list of some of the largest and/or most unusual of the cable networks.

ARTS (Alpha Repertory Television Service)
Hearst/ABC Video
555 Fifth Ave.
New York, NY 10017
212-661-4500
Cultural programming with occasional "Masterpiece Theatre" reruns and other British fare.

BET (Black Entertainment Television)
1050 31st St. NW
Washington, DC 20007
202-337-5260
Films, musical specials, sports, etc. that would be of particular interest to a black audience.

CBN (Christian Broadcasting Network)
CBN Center
1000 Centerville Turnpike
Virginia Beach, VA 23463
804-424-7777
Religious programming, some family entertainment.

CHN (Cable Health Network)
9356 Little Santa Monica Blvd.
Beverly Hills, CA 90210
213-550-7230
Health and "life-style" programming.

CNN (Cable News Network)
1050 Techwood Dr. NW
Atlanta, GA 30318
404-898-8500
Round-the-clock news. One of the most successful of the cable networks.

C-SPAN (Cable Satellite Public Affairs Network)
400 N. Capitol St. NW
Washington, DC 20001
202-737-3220
Live and taped coverage of congressional debates and hearings and some viewer call-in shows with government officials.

The Disney Channel
4111 West Alameda Ave.
Burbank, CA 91505
818-846-6661
Disney features and other family entertainment.

ESPN (Entertainment and Sports Programming Network)
ESPN Plaza
Bristol, CT 06010
203-584-8477
Sports and sports news around the clock.

HBO (Home Box Office)
1271 Sixth Ave.
New York, NY 10017
212-484-1000
The first and still the biggest pay TV service.

MTV (Music Television)
Warner/Amex Satellite Entertainment Co.
1133 Avenue of the Americas
New York, NY 10036
212-944-5398
Music videos and news around the clock. One of the most innovative and successful of all the cable networks.

The Nashville Network
2806 Opryland Dr.
Nashville, TN 37214
615-889-6840
Country music and variety shows.

Nickelodeon
1133 Sixth Ave.
New York, NY 10036
212-944-5521
Children's programming.

NJT (National Jewish Television)
2621 Palisades Ave.
Riverdale, NY 10463
212-549-4160
Programming for a Jewish audience.

PTL (Praise The Lord)
7224 Park Rd.
Charlotte, NC 28279
704-542-6000
Christian programming.

Showtime
1633 Broadway
New York, NY 10019
212-708-1600
Next to HBO, the largest pay TV entertainment network.

SIN (National Spanish Television Network)
250 Park Ave.
New York, NY 10017
212-953-7507
Spanish-language programming.

SPN (Satellite Program Network)
PO Box 45684
Tulsa, OK 74175
918-481-0881
Wide variety of low-budget "life-style" programming aimed primarily at women.

USA Cable Network
208 Harristown Rd.
Glen Rock, NJ 07452
210-445-8550
A wide variety of programming from children's programs and wrestling to Andy Warhol movies on "Night Flight."

The Weather Channel
2625 Cumberland Parkway
Atlanta, GA 30339
404-434-6800
Weather reports around the clock.

In addition to the cable networks there are several "distant signal channels" or "superstations." These are local stations beamed by satellite throughout the country.

WGN (Chicago)
5200 Harvard
Tulsa, OK 74135
800-331-4806

WOR (New York) Eastern Microwave
112 Northern Concourse
PO Box 4872
Syracuse, NY 13221
315-455-5955

WTBS (Atlanta)
1050 Techwood Dr. N.W.
Atlanta, GA 30318
404-898-8500

THE LARGEST CABLE SYSTEM OPERATORS

American TV & Communications Corp.
160 Inverness Dr. West
Englewood, CO 80112
303-773-3411

Cablevisions Systems Development Co.
1 Media Crossways Dr.
Woodbury, NY 11797
516-364-8450

Capital Cities Communication
7120 E. Orchard Rd.
Englewood, CO 80111
303-770-7500

Central Communications Corp.
993 Oak St.
Aurora, IL 60506
312-897-2288

Century Communications Corp.
51 Locust Ave.
New Canaan, CT 96840
203-966-8746

Colony Communications, Inc.
PO Box 969
Providence, RI 02901
401-277-7444

Comcast Corp.
1 Belmont Ave., Suite 227
Bala Cynwyd, PA 19004
215-667-4200

Communications Services, Inc.
100 Rimrock, Box 829
Junction City, KS 66441
913-762-2670

Continental Cablevision, Inc.
Lewis Wharf, Pilot House
Boston, MA 02110
617-742-9500

Cox Cable Communications, Inc.
219 Perimeter Center Parkway
Atlanta, GA 30346
404-393-0480

Daniels & Associates, Inc.
2930 E. Third Ave., Box 6008
Denver, CO 80206
303-321-7550

General Electric Cablevision Inc.
1400 Balltown Rd.
Schenectady, NY 12309
518-385-1368

Group W Cable
888 Seventh Ave.
New York, NY 10016
212-247-8700

Harron Communications Corp.
2063 Suburban Station Bldg.
Philadelphia, PA 19103
215-569-2935

Heritage Communications, Inc.
2195 Ingersoll Ave.
Des Moines, IA 50312
515-245-7585

Jones Intercable, Inc.
5275 DTC Parkway
Englewood, CO 80111
303-740-9700

Liberty Communications, Inc.
225 Coburg Rd.
Eugene, OR 94701
503-485-5611

McLean Hunter
27 Faskin Dr.
Rexdale, Ontario, Canada
416-675-5930

Multimedia Cablevision, Inc.
140 W. 9th
Cincinnati, OH 45202
513-352-5000

Newchannels Corp.
112 Northern Concourse,
PO Box 4872
Syracuse, NY 13221
315-455-5826

Prime Cable Corp.
1515 City National Bank Bldg.
Austin, TX 78701
512-476-7888

Rogers/UA Cablesystems
315 Post Rd. West
Westport, CT 06880
203-227-9581

Sammons Communications
500 S. Ervay, Box 225728
Dallas, TX 75002
214-742-9828

Service Electric Cable TV, Inc.
1403 Hamilton St.
Allentown, PA 18101
215-827-7750

Storer Cable Communications
1177 Kane Concourse
Miami Beach, FL 33154
305-866-0211

Telecable Corp.
740 Duke St., Box 720
Norfolk, VA 23510
804-446-2565

Tele-Communications, Inc.
5455 S. Valentia Way
Englewood, CO 80111
303-771-8200

Tele-Media Corp.
PO Box 39
Bellfont, PA 16823
814-237-1512

Texas Community Antenna Group
PO Box 6840
Tyler, TX 75711
214-595-3701

Times Mirror Cablevision
2381 Morse Ave., Box 19398
Irvine, CA 92713
714-549-2173

United Cable TV Corp.
Terminal Annex, Box 5840
Denver, CO 80217
303-779-5999

Viacom Communications
1211 Sixth Ave.
New York, NY 10036
212-575-5175

Warner/Amex Cable Communications, Inc.
75 Rockefeller Plaza
New York, NY 10019
212-484-8000

Western Communications, Inc.
PO Box 4610
Walnut Creek, CA 94596
415-935-3055

Wometco Communications, Inc.
316 N. Miami Ave.
Miami, FL 33128
303-579-1200

INDEX

Italicized page numbers refer to illustrations.

Account executives, 69
Ace Award, 78
Advertising, 25, 62
Announcers, 36
Archaeology, 61
Art directors, 70
Audio/video engineers, 40
Audio-visual (AV) clubs, 54, 84
Audio-visual education, 63–64

"Basement Tapes," 14
Baxter, Tracy, 22–23
"A Better Way," 67, 69
"Bicycling," 52
"The Big Giveaway," 51

Buggles, The, 17
Cable Fact Book, 52
Cable networks, 100–104
Cable News Network (CNN), 25, 29, *38*
Cable 6, 19–20, 22, 24, 40, 43–44
Cable system operators, 104–108
Cable television, 9, 11, 19–33, 43
    public-access channels, 44–52
    subscription services, 24, 32
Camera operators, 39
Carson, Johnny, 9, 50
CATV (Community Antenna Television), 26

Christian Broadcasting Network, 29
Cincinnati, University of, 72
Closed-circuit TV, 64, 66–67, 78
Coaxial cable, 19
Colleges, 72, 90–96
College television studios, 64
Collins, Michael, 11–12, 73
Commercials, 20, 36
Communications satellites, 26
Community colleges, 72
Corporate communications, 61
Country music videos, 17
Creative writing jobs, 69

Della-Guistina, Marsha, 78
DeMond, Calvin, 20–23
Directors, 39–40
Direct Satellite Broadcast, 32
Dish antennas, 32
"Down to Earth," 69

Editing, 40, *75, 76*
Egan, Mike, 24
Emerson College, *35*, 74, 78, *80*, 81–82
Emerson Independent Videos (EIV), 78, 81–82
Employee-orientation, 61
Engineering degrees, 24–25
"The English Channel," 51
ESPN, 19–20, 25, *31, 37, 41*

Experimental videos, 59, *75, 83*
EVVY awards, *80*

Farming videos, 67–69
Fine arts videos, 61
"Friday Night Video Fights," 14

Game shows, 50–51
General Electric, 29
Government videos, 67–69
Grants, 98–99
Graphic artists, 40, 42

Harris, Ellen Stern, 49
Headend, 24
Home Box Office (HBO), 19, 26–30
Hospital videos, 64–67

Installers, 24
Insurance documentation, 60–61
Interactive television, 30, 32
"International Championship Wrestling," 20
Internships, 21–23, 81–82, 96–98
Interviewers, 36

Journalism, degrees in, 23

"Karen's Restaurant Revue," 50
Kovacs, Ernie, 21
Kramer, Jerry, 56, 71, 85

Lighting directors, 40

— 110 —

Live Aid concert, 12–13
Local origination channels, 43–44

"The Making of Thriller," 56, 71
Manhattan Cable TV, 45–46
Marketing, 25
Medical videos, 64–67
Microwave TV, 66
"Midnight Blue," 45
Military videos, 82, 84
Minow, Newton, 26
"Mom-and-Pop" cable systems, 26
Moore, Steve, 73–77
Murrow, Edward R., 21
Music Television (MTV), 9–20, 25, 29, *58*

Newhouse, S.I. *See* Syracuse University
News reporting, 22–23
New York University, 73
"Night Flight," 17
"Nonlinear approach," 12
Nontechnical jobs, 40, 42
North Carolina, University of, 74

Obscenity, 46
Ohio University, 74
Oil well videos, 61
Orange County Cablevision, 19, 25

Pasadena City College, 72
Patents, videos for, 60–61
Patient education, 66

Performers, 36, 43–52
Playboy Channel, 29, 45
Political videos, 61
Pornography, 45
Producers, 69
Producing amateur videos, 47, 49–52
Product demos, 61–62
Project ideas, 49–52
"Promos," 12
Public-access cable TV, 43–52
Public information, videos for, 67
Public relations, 43–52, 70

Racetrack videos, 61
"Radio 1990," 17
Regional networks, 51
Reruns, 30
Rock music cable channels, 9
"Rock Rock Rock," 14
Rock videos, 13
Rosenthal, Arnie, 50–51
Roth, David Lee, 71

Salkin, Karen, 50
Sarnoff, David, 21
Satellite Communications, *27*, *28*, 32. *See also* Home Box Office
Satellites and dish antennas, 32
Scholarships, 96–99
"Scrambling" signals, 32
Security systems, videos for, 61
Senior producers, 70
Showtime, 19
Sportscasters, 34, 36

Sports refereeing, 61
Stagehands, 42
Stereo link-up, 13-14
Still cameras, 54
Studio work, 34-42
Syndicated cable TV, 20
Syracuse University, 74-78, *83*

Taping services, 57
Technical jobs, 24-25
Technology, video, 11-12
Teleconference development specialists, 70
Television franchises, 29
Television performers, 36, 43-52
Television writing, 40, 42
Texas, University of, 74
Trade magazines, 62-63, 86-88
Trade schools, 72
Training films, 61-67
Two-way television, 30, 32, 66
Two-year programs, 72

"The Ugly George Hour of Truth, Sex and Violence," 45-46
Unit managers, 40
University of California, Los Angeles, 73
USA Network, 17
US Department of Agriculture, 67-69

"Vanity Videos," 52
Variety, 36
VH-I, 17
Video cameras, 54-59

Video careers, 11, 20-23, 54-59, 69-70
 education for, 71-85
 as engineers, 40
 pressures in, 18
 as technicians, 69
 as VJs, 9, 11, 34
Video cassette recorders (VCRs), 53-54
Video, education in, 63-64, 71-85
Video equipment, 53-59
"Video fluency," 12
Video jockeys (VJs), 9, 11, 34
"Video Killed the Radio Star," 17
Video production units, 67
Video research, 77-78
Video Soul, *16*
Videotape engineers, 40
Videotapes, uses of, 11, 60-70
Video technicians, 69
Video yearbooks, 63
Volunteer work, 21-23, 46-47, *48*, 84

Warner/Amex Satellite Entertainment Company, 17, 29, 78
Weather Channel, 25
Weather forecasting, 36
Wells, Tamara, 18, 81
Wisconsin, University of, 74
Woodstock concert, 13
Workshops, 46
Worley, Marianne, 22-23

Yellin, Tom, 12